WAR OF THE WILLS

by

Catherine McLeod

Catherine McLeod

In loving memory of
Kim Short
30/4/1959 – 19/1/2016

8 WILLS
The Catherine McLeod Story
By MAREE FURNISS

Eight Wills made, eight Wills played Family and money don't mix so well
A dead person ignored because they can't tell The truth of their wishes the truth of their Will And the family like vultures they take their fill Of the land, the money and all of the treasure
They steal the spoils, for their own selfish pleasure And the one who mattered
The one who cared They cast her aside
As if she too, were dead.

Catherine McLeod

∞

WAR OF THE WILLS

by

Catherine McLeod

Copyright © Catherine McLeod - 2017

CATHERINE MCLEOD *asserts the moral right to be identified as the author of this work*

The National Library of Australia Cataloguing in Publication

Author: McLeod – Catherine

Title: War of the Wills

ISBN: 978-0-6481087-0-2

All rights Reserved

No part of this book may be reproduced in any form by photocopying or by any electronic or mechanical means, including information storage or retrieval systems without permission in writing from the Author and the publisher of this book the publisher of this book.

This book is based on actual events. The Author has changed names and taken all care to protect the identities of people including identity within scenarios mentioned in this publication.

Book cover design by The Book Design House

www.thebookdesignhouse.com

Table of Contents

1. The History of Allen and May
2. Allen Embarks on a New Career
3. How I Met Allen
4. Life with May
5. Other Ventures
6. May has a Bung Ticker
7. May is Dying
8. Life after May
9. Early Signs of Ill Health
10. Allen Gets Sick
11. Life with a Parkinson's Person
12. Allen Making Wills
13. 1999 Allen's Disease takes over his Life
14. Allen Becomes Impossible to Manage
15. Allen Needs More Help
16. Allen's Health Declines Even Further
17. Allen Goes to Live in a Nursing Home
18. Another Will
19. The War Begins
20. The Lying Begins
21. Yet Another Will
22. More Wills Being Made
23. Diary Notes Written during the Last Few Months of Allen's Life

24. That Final Will
25. The End is Nigh for Allen
26. Allen Dies
27. Learning About Handwriting and Signatures
28. Beryl Takes Control of the Assets
29. Notes from My Diary
30. I Get a Flat Car Tyre. And Again! And Again! And Again...!
31. There's Something Wrong with the Water
32. The Pick Up
33. I Get Pulled up by the Police
34. The Undertaking Agreement to Leave Me Alone!!!
35. The Harassment Continues in a Different Form; Strange Telephone Calls
36. Some Unusual People Become Part of My Life
37. The End is in Sight--Maybe!
38. More Intimidation: The Drive-bys
39. Another Mediation
40. A Time to Spy
41. A New Tactic for Me
42. The Case Moves a Little Forward
43. Proving Allen's Lack of Mental Lucidity
44. If You Throw Enough Mud at a Wall, some of it May Stick
45. Mediation Number Four: The Final One
46. The Making of the Final Will Explained

47. Fighting Back

48. A Settlement is Reached

Connect with Catherine McLeod

1. The History of Allen and May

Allen and May's story began early last century before I, Catherine McLeod, was even born. Allen Desmond Johnson was born to wealthy parents. His father General Allen Johnson was a First World War veteran and his mother was a Melbourne business woman, Melissa Magda Johnson. The last of a line of Allen Johnsons, although he had the addition of Desmond as his middle name, he was educated at a prestigious Melbourne private school. As could be expected of a man with his background, he had a true gentlemanly demeanour about him.

An avid sportsman, like his forebears, he held championship titles for boxing, running and rowing. He also played football and had a keen interest in many other sports. I often reflected on his boxing competitions and wondered whether they in some way contributed to him developing Parkinson's disease later in life. Although Dux of his class in form V with his school report for that year being excellent, the next year his report had him barely passing his subjects. He blamed this on the Second World War, during which he considered the standard of his education had deteriorated.

He felt that all the good young teachers were off fighting and the only teachers left were crusty, stale old men who had been seconded from retirement to fill the teaching vacancies.

As his academic achievements diminished during the war years he lost interest in his schooling. Much to the disappointment of his parents, who wanted him to go to university, he got a job after completing year twelve. Wanting to join the army and become a soldier, he was too young to enlist without his parent's permission, although he was in the Senior Cadets Corps with his school. His parents would not allow him to enlist, so he did not get to fight in the war. He deeply regretted this in later life, as returned soldiers received a war service pension if they managed to survive until they reached pension age of sixty years. He would often lament the fact that many men he knew got a war pension with all its inherent benefits and yet he couldn't. My suggestion that he might have been killed if he had been fighting in the war, and thus would still have missed out on getting the pension, was not agreed with as he claimed that all the fighting was over by the time he wanted to enlist, and the soldiers were mainly used for peacekeeping forces. I still thought that there was the possibility he might have died.

Even though his parents had other ambitions for him, Allen chose to work as a stockman on a couple of sheep and cattle stations. The first was Silver Falls Estate in northern Victoria, the second- Warrytree Station in southern New South Wales. After about a year he decided that station work was not to his liking. The weather was always either unbearably hot and dusty or wet, muddy and freezing cold, depending on the time of year and the season. The work days were very long and extremely hard. As part of his job he had to handle and ride some very intractable horses and he regularly fell off and hurt himself. If that wasn't bad enough, he also had to avoid certain male co-workers who made unwanted advances at night due to his attractiveness! When he first arrived at the stations some of the men that he was working with warned him about which men he had to watch out for if he did not wish to be molested. Of course, he kept this information in mind throughout his station employment! After he resigned from the Warrytree station job he returned to Melbourne and bought his own farm at Smith's Gully, a small town north of Melbourne, where he raised sheep.

He made quite a success of his first farming enterprise and was able to own his farm outright in twelve months, after the sale of the bales of wool from his first year's wool shearing. He was quite proud of himself and regularly boasted about that little entrepreneurial success. Smith's Gully in the late 1940s was considered quite remote and farms in the area were very cheap to buy so a large return wasn't needed from the wool to cover the purchase price of the farm.

Whilst working on his Smith's Gully farm he was visited by some of his friends and introduced to his future wife, May Ridge, who was newly free after her war romance engagement to an American naval officer had broken down. Allen and May had a fond, affectionate relationship for a few years before they got married in 1951. He claimed that he wasn't keen to get married because she was older than him, but May talked him into it. She was from the seaside suburb of Brighton and was an attractive young Melbourne socialite, whose parents ran a successful button importing company. She certainly was a good catch based on her family background. They spent their first few years of married life on farms that Allen owned, first on the farm at Smith's Gully and later at a place called Clarkfield. Both were located about a one-hour drive north of Melbourne. It does not sound like a great distance today but in the early 1950s people considered it to be a full-day excursion to go from the city to the farm to visit them. They started a Jersey cow dairy where they milked cows, chopped firewood to sell in the winter, and kept sheep and pigs.

Not a person to dispose of things willy-nilly, at the time of his death Allen still had a diary given to him and May some fifty-five years earlier by the previous owners of the Clarkfield farm. It was a very detailed almanac on the running of the farm with the dates on which they should do various annual activities. The first entry for the first Monday in January was thus notated: "usually a day of rest after a strenuous harvest." Tuesday, however, had the farmers back at hard labour. The Tuesday entry: "Commence cutting maize (corn) one big armful per cow. Usually do this after breakfast and distribute it around the paddock." Keep in mind they were out early milking the cows before breakfast! "Place sheep on rape paddock. Cut Scotch Thistles before they can flower or seed and commence spraying blackberries with any hormone spray. Cut any docks before they seed."

The diary continues giving dates to mate the cows, pigs and sheep, as well as when various other farm chores needed to be done. It finishes with a page of information on how May should fill in her day working on the farm. One can only imagine the thoughts that would have been going through the minds of her parents when they visited her on the farm. Their precious daughter, who was raised to be the lady of a household, was working as a farm navvy. Allen also played football for the local football club, where he seemed to sustain several broken bones, including his ribs, which left him with a misshapen chest for the rest of his life. May did the cow milking and tended to the animals while he was off playing football and when he was convalescing from his injuries.

Allen always thought that his father-in-law was disappointed with his daughter's choice of a husband. Her previous fiancé, the American Naval Captain, was from a wealthy Southern US family, and Allen described him as the closest that America had to royalty. As a young woman May never had to learn to cook or do housework because her family had servants to cook and clean the house. In keeping with elite English tradition, they changed clothes in the evening and dressed up to eat dinner. Her parents were English migrants who came to Australia because of her father's health problems. He had been advised by his doctor to move to a warmer climate. An Australian man who put his daughter to work on a farm milking cows and chopping wood seemed a dismal second choice compared to the life of luxurious opulence, shopping and spending the husband's family wealth as she would have had with her previous fiancé. May never expressed any regret about becoming a farming wife. Allen said that she never wanted to talk about it so it was never discussed. The couple's only child, Beryl, was born about six years into their marriage, while they were still farming at Clarkfield. Allen didn't want any more children so she was an only child.

Allen's family were wealthy also and they had a maid to do the chores around the house, but his family was a little more Australianised and did not dress up every day to eat dinner. Although his mother was English, his father's family was Australian-born. One comment he made about the maids that worked for his family was that he didn't know whether it was by coincidence or design but the maids were always extraordinarily ugly. It was a most interesting observation for a young boy to make. He did not take up the tradition of having household help for May. She had to do the household chores herself, including learning how to cook.

Allen's father-in-law was not entirely happy about his daughter working so hard on a farm, particularly after the birth of her baby girl. He encouraged them to move back to Melbourne to live. The Clarkfield farm was sold and they bought a house in Mentone, one of

Melbourne's south-eastern suburbs. It was suggested by the father-in-law that Allen should invest some of the proceeds from the sale of the farm into his button company and work for him. He was to have a managerial role although he soon found that he had to start at the bottom of the company as a travelling salesman selling buttons and other haberdashery items. He hated the job. The last straw for him was when he walked into a shop in a Victorian country town where the woman shopkeeper asked him whether he had any 'Mother of Pearl' buttons. He did not have a clue what they were and told me, "I went out to the car and got all of the button samples that I had and threw them at her. I said, 'Here pick the ones that you want from these!'" It became apparent there was no immediate managerial role forthcoming. To add insult to injury the money that he had invested into the company was issued as company shares to May, solely in her name.

Allen went from being a financially independent, self-employed master of his own domain to being trapped as a lackey to his father-in-law. His money was now his wife's, so he could not easily pack up and go. He never got over that little deception and often complained about his cunning father- in-law and how he had tricked him. To her credit, his wife had advised him not to do it; he should have paid more attention to her! This event made him very cautious in his dealings with future business partners.

2. Allen Embarks on a New Career

Allen did not last very long working for his father-in-law and soon moved on to try his luck in other businesses. He had to begin again from scratch, this time with a wife and child to support, and he tried his hand at a few things. Bookmaking was one of them, the betting kind of bookmaker, not a person who makes a book to read. However, his major focus was in real estate, where he was quite successful. In addition to working as an agent selling properties for others, he bought old houses suitable for demolition on large developable blocks of land. He built flats and offices on these properties and he told me many stories of the difficulties he encountered with local councils, convincing them that his development proposal was a suitable proposition for the area. He had to deal with objections from local residents and provide convincing arguments to get many of his developments approved. Many legal battles occurred when he was in business as a Real Estate Agent and Property Developer. I loved hearing about his property development stories and found these conversations fascinating.

His real estate agency was in the suburb of Sandringham, a beachside suburb in the south east of Melbourne. He traded in properties, mostly in Melbourne's eastern suburbs; however, he always retained his penchant for having a farm. He bought a farm at Loch, about an hour and a half drive from the city, on Melbourne's south east. At the Loch property, he spent many weekends camping with an old bachelor neighbour Howard, in Howard's rough dwelling that he had built with his own hands. His mother visited the farm soon after he bought it. She shook her head and told him to give up and go and play golf.

Her son did not take her advice and a few months after he bought his property, he decided to put a house on it so that May and Beryl could come and spend weekends there with him. He had previously purchased a valuable block of land in the Bayside suburb of Carrum, where an older style seaside cottage was already constructed, although he wanted to remove it so that he could build apartments on the land. Wanting a weekend house on his Loch property, he decided that he could move his seaside cottage onto the farm.

Moving a complete house required a number of different government permits, all of which would take quite a few months to obtain. Allen wanted his seaside block of land cleared quickly and knew a man who owned a low loader truck, the sort that is used to move houses. He got another friend to help him jack the house onto the low loader to move it. As he didn't have any road transport permits and didn't want to wait, they moved the house in the middle of the night to avoid detection. Unfortunately, they forgot to check the heights of the overhead electricity power lines along the way, although if he had obtained a road transport permit, he would have been given a planned route. He took the most direct route and, to his shock, discovered that some of the electric power lines were hanging lower than the height of the house! As they drove he said that they saw sparks shooting out from the roof of the house as it scraped under a few sets of power lines causing the wires to touch each other and spark. It looked spectacular, like a fireworks display. They were lucky that they didn't get electrocuted!

Finally, they got to the farm without any further drama, and he ended up with his weekender. The house was always pointed out to me whenever we drove past that farm. He was very proud of it. When I looked at the house I thought of his story about how he moved it to the property and visualized sparks shooting out from the roof.

Allen kept his friendship with old Howard long after he sold his own property at Loch. Whenever we drove past the farm we would often call in at Howard's place to visit him. His farm was a sight to behold. Howard had ducks! It seemed like he had thousands of them and he bought sacks of stale bread from the Dandenong livestock auction sale yards for their feed. The place was a mélange of plastic bread wrappers and duck excrement. It took great intestinal fortitude to drink a cup of tea at Howard's. I always managed not to be hungry while I was there; however, Allen happily feasted on whatever was offered. He would tell me stories of the mealtimes that he had at Howard's when he had stayed there in the past. Howard would scrape out the mouldy remains from his mixing bowl and saucepan and proceed to reuse the items without any thought of washing them. "The cooking destroyed the germs," he would say. Even though Allen sold his Loch property and bought his next farm in Cranbourne, he remained in regular contact with Howard until he died.

The Cranbourne farm is also in Melbourne's south east but much closer to the city. It was about a 40-minute drive from his home in Sandringham and about the same distance from the Brighton house, where they lived when May inherited it from her parents after they died. A couple of years later Allen bought another farm on the opposite side of the road. The second farm is the one where I now live. He bought this farm jointly with his wife. May contributed $15,000 of the purchase price using the share dividend proceeds that she received from the family company shares that he had paid for and he paid the balance of $63,000. He now had two properties in Cranbourne.

In the late 1970s and early 1980s May lived mostly at her house in Brighton, where Beryl and her family now live, and Allen alternated between living in the house on the first Cranbourne farm and the Brighton house. The Brighton house was built by May's father and she was born in it. She was very proud of the fact that it was the place where she was born. Her mother did not go to hospital to have her but delivered her baby with the aid of a midwife in her own bed in the bedroom. When her parents died she received the house and its contents, as well as further shares in her father's button company. She and her sister each received half of their father's shareholding in the company. May loved her Brighton home and I feel sure that it would have suited her to die there when her time came. Allen hated the drive back and forth and complained bitterly whenever necessity compelled him to drive there for the night. He pfererred to stay on the farm.

When I first met Allen in the late 1970s his daughter was a University student and lived in one of the Melbourne University student accommodation Colleges. She would come down to the farm to go horse riding on the weekends. Later her future husband, Wayne Bilk, became a regular visitor. Allen never warmed to him, and was critical of him right from the beginning, often complaining that he only latched onto his daughter because the parents had money. May did not agree with this premise and she always said that they were a couple who were well suited to each other. It seemed obvious that Wayne was the more dominant personality. Beryl had a strong will but she gave in to him whenever there was conflict between them. They married in the early 1980s and set up house in Brighton, close to where May lived. They regularly visited her in the evenings at her home.

In 1982 the directors of the Ridge family button company wanted to buy out May's shares in the company. Allen was pressing for her to sell the shares and use the money to invest in real estate. She consulted Wayne about the offer and he got a financial adviser to assess the company's value. As the situation was described to me, Wayne felt that May's shareholding was being undervalued because the company held import licences and the imputed value of these licences was not being considered at the time.

These import licences meant that the company had the right to import buttons from other countries and had a monopoly in this field. At that time, Australian businesses needed a licence to import goods from another country, and importing was strictly controlled by the Australian government. Allen did not agree with this, as he felt the value of the shares would drop because the government was planning to remove the import protection from Australian industries to make Australia more competitive on the world market. When this happened, anyone could import whatever they wanted from other countries, forcing businesses in Australia to be more competitive with each other.

An Australian business that had an import licence could no longer charge whatever they wanted for their imported stock, as other companies could import for themselves at a lower price and sell their imported goods for less. At Wayne's instigation, a report was prepared for May and a letter written suggesting that she should not sell her shares just then. Allen was very angry with Wayne because he had to pay for the report, which he did not request. He also recognised that Wayne was going over his head by giving May advice on shares that he had previously paid for. He believed that he should have the say over what happened to the shares. He felt that she could do as she pleased with the shares that her father gave her in his estate but the other shares should have been a joint decision between them both. As things turned out, Allen was right and Wayne was wrong. The family company shares fell in value while real estate prices skyrocketed. From then on, he constantly made critical comments about Wayne's business acumen to May and me.

Wayne was an accountant, as was his father, who had an office in Collingwood, a suburb of Melbourne just north of the city. Beryl often suggested to her father that he should get him to do his accountancy work, as he was very clever. She found that she was paying very little tax after she married him and he started doing her tax returns, compared to the amount of tax that she was paying before she met him. Allen was not interested in changing accountants, no matter how critical his daughter was of his own. He still preferred his existing accountant and steadfastly refused to hand over his business bookkeeping to Wayne.

3. How I Met Allen

Allen and I met through a man who worked with my husband. They had a few horses, as did a few the men who worked with him. The horse fraternity at his work tended to keep company with each other and also socialised as family groups. They often did horse-related activities together and went trail riding. This man bought a horse that May had advertised for sale in the paper, and my husband went with him to help bring the horse to his own farm in a horse float. This was in about 1977, when my husband, our son and I lived in South Dandenong. I was quite happy living there.

We had sixteen acres of land around the house, which was a good size to keep our horses, along with good neighbours and had established a nice little social group around us. The place where we lived was for sale and I wanted us to buy it. We had enough money for a deposit and we both had good jobs, but my husband always saw the grass as being greener on the other side of the fence and wanted to move to the house on the property where Allen and May kept the horse they had sold.

That is the farm where I now live. At the time, there was a tenant in the house but my husband asked to be informed when the tenant moved out, because he wanted to rent the house and live there. I felt that the place was in the middle of nowhere and wasn't very keen to move. In 1977 Cranbourne certainly was a very small place but it was very peaceful to go horse riding as cars rarely drove by, which is why it appealed to my husband.

In 1978 the house became vacant and we ended up moving. I had to give up my job that I really enjoyed. Although I did not smoke, I worked as a cigarette sample distributor. It was fun, paid well and was easy to do, travelling around giving away free cigarettes. I was very disappointed, having to give up that job, but it would have been impossible for me to continue. I had a child in school and the extra time and distance in travelling each day would have left me no time for other things.

The property had a few large sheds on it. An earlier tenant on the property was a racehorse trainer and had converted the insides of the sheds into horse stables. My husband decided that I should educate and train horses to make a living for myself, using the horse facilities on the property. I worked hard at this venture and May and Allen seemed to enjoy giving me assistance whenever they could. May did not work in paid employment and Allen had retired from active work as a real estate agent. They spent their time running the farms and looking after his investment properties, so they were able to spend a lot of time with me and my horses.

He had cattle on both of his farms, and I regularly rode a horse around the properties helping them to herd the cattle. It was good exercise for the horses and it was fun, so I looked forward to doing it. Although May had been a keen equestrian in the past, she rarely rode when I knew her. She had a bad car accident some years previously and seriously injured her knee, which never fully healed, making it painful for her to ride. She also suffered from shortness of breath which became very pronounced when she did any physical work, especially horse riding. She either walked around the properties or drove in a small utility.

The country move was not helpful to my marriage, and my husband and I parted soon after. I bought a house nearby and moved out while he continued to live on the property. I studied part time for an Arts Degree, followed by a Diploma in Education. During this time I kept in regular contact with Allen and May while I continued to rent the stables for my horse training.

4. Life with May

After my marriage breakdown my life was very enjoyable. My not contact University days were spent on the farm with the animals. Allen and I had a similar sense of humour and found many things to laugh and joke about. Although May could never get the humour in many of his jokes, she was still a cheerful person to be around. He was a great one for seeing the funny side of things and loved to recount incidents that he found funny. One very funny time for him was when his daughter was sending out wedding invitations for her impending marriage. He had a lovely handwriting style and was given the task of writing on the invitation cards. This was in the pre-computer era when people would hand-write on cards. On this particular day, he was seated at the kitchen table writing guest's names on the pre-printed wedding invitation cards when a young tabby cat called Tibbles, who was extremely unwell with diarrhoea, walked into the kitchen. Tibbles was stick thin, literally skin covering bones with an ungroomed coat of matted hair. She was one of May's favourites. May had tried in vain to groom her and cure her ailments. Tibbles or Tibby as she was often called was special enough to be allowed into the house.

The wedding card story as told to me by a laughing Allen:

"There I was sitting at the table writing on the cards when Tibbles jumped up onto the table. Beryl as quick as a flash grabbed Tibby around her middle before she could walk on the cards and leave dirty paw prints on them. Tibby got such a shock at being suddenly grabbed that she squirted shit out of her arse all over the cards. There were small spatters of shit all over just about every card, and Beryl was distraught.

We tried to clean the cards but there were small brown dots all over them. Beryl declared that the cards all stank of cat shit and had to be thrown away." Allen loved telling the cat story to anyone who would listen and laugh. New invitation cards were purchased!

At any one time, there would be a dozen or so cats on the farm that were sick with flu or diarrhoea as May kept cats. A very large number of cats! Most of them lived outside around the farm, a lot of them sheltered in the hay shed. The bales of hay would have vast numbers of cats perched on them. I always chuckled when visitors commented on the cats.

"There are a lot of cats here!" They would state. I always thought that was an understatement. About twenty or so were considered special enough to be allowed to live inside the house. Allen was always asking May, "What makes this cat better than the ones in the hay shed? Why is it allowed to come inside and not the others?" She could never explain the reason to him and I doubt that she knew the answer.

5. Other Ventures

Being a licenced Real Estate Agent, Allen was very interested in the property market. He spent many hours reading through all the newspaper real estate for sale sections looking for potential property bargains. This was in the days before computers and Internet property listings. Whenever he read an advertisement for a farm for sale that seemed interesting to him, the three of us would go for a drive to check out the property. We had many fun drives checking out deserted farmhouses in various stages of dilapidation. The houses always had overgrown gardens, often with unusual plants growing in them. May was a keen gardener so plant cuttings often returned home with us. I have a mass of bulbs that flower brilliant orange flowers every year. They are the offspring of one bulb from an old farmhouse garden that is now a road.

I would accompany him in his cattle transport truck to cattle and sheep sales but May rarely joined us. She found it very uninteresting. On sale mornings, he would come to my place and we would eat breakfast together while I got my son ready for school. We ate toast with homemade cumquat marmalade as he regularly made large batches of the marmalade whenever the cumquat tree in his garden bore fruit. He would drink a cup of tea into which he added a quarter teaspoon of Kruschen Salts. I only knew about this product from the television commercials when I was a child. 'Get that Kruschen Feeling', it said in the advertisement. He was the first and only person that I had ever seen using the stuff, and told me it was excellent for keeping the bowels regular. "It makes you shit like a thousand arrows," he would say. On hearing this, I was never tempted to try it.

On Tuesdays Allen and I would go to the Newmarket sheep sales in Melbourne. It was located close to the city, adjacent to an abattoir. The Newmarket sale yard no longer exists as it was closed down in 1987, along with the abattoir. The whole Newmarket sale yard and abattoir area is now an up-market residential suburb. Over the years he bought thousands of sheep from the sale yards that were there. I cannot describe how much I enjoyed the trip across town to Newmarket with him. We always seemed to find so much to talk about while driving. The trip involved driving along a road that ran beside the Yarra River in Melbourne City past some of the prestigious Melbourne private schools such as Scotch College, and St Kevin's College. Early in the morning the river near the city was alive with activity. There were students from those schools rowing in their skiffs up and down the river. Most were training for rowing competitions. There were various configurations of skiffs and crew members in them. While we were driving past he would explain to me about the way that the rowing teams worked and how the competitions were held. He talked about his school days, when he rowed, and the wins that he had when he was a teenager. He was part of a crew that won a big rowing competition for his school. The win gave the rowers a lot of kudos; it was even featured in a Melbourne newspaper with photos. Allen was a sporting hero on that day.

When we arrived at the sale yards we walked around looking for potential sheep to buy. Allen always bought to a budget and wanted bargain- priced animals. He tended to buy the cheapest that he could find, which turned out to be animals that were either, very small and young or very thin and barely alive. The good thing about sheep is that they are tough. They could be so emaciated that they could hardly walk from weakness but after a couple of weeks in a paddock that had a little green grass they would become fat and lively.

We enjoyed the challenge of finding suitable animals for us to purchase. He relied on my animal appraising skills to help him decide on which animals to bid on. I seemed to have a knack for weeding out the diseased looking creatures from the healthy but hungry animals. I could smell footrot and other ailments on the sheep. Many people did not believe it but when I looked at a pen of sheep and said that I could smell footrot on them when someone checked the feet on those sheep they always had footrot. There were thousands of sheep on any sale day. There were usually thirty to fifty animals penned together in small corrals. Each corral would have animals that were similar in size and age. They would also be sorted by their weight. Fat sheep would be penned together and thin sheep would be together in another pen. We would have to check through the sheep in a pen to see that the majority appeared to be healthy. It was one thing to buy thin sheep but they had to be still strong enough to survive, which was not always the case with animals at a sale.

In addition to butchers looking to buy fat lambs that were to be slaughtered and sold as meat in their shops, there were farmers and sheep traders there. The latter were looking to buy bargain-priced sheep to fatten on their farms or for resale to people who had farms but no time to spend at auction sales themselves. The traders were the bane of Allen's sheep buying life. He would comment on the way home after a sale, "If only 'x' hadn't been there or 'y' hadn't turned up today, I would have bought some bargains." I would say to him, "If x and y stopped coming there would be fifty more bargain sheep buyers there to take their places. There will always be someone else."

Having purchased his truck load of sheep, we herded them along the laneways between the pens to an area where the livestock transport trucks were parked. This was often a very tricky process due to the small size of many of the lambs that he had bought. The little creatures could dissolve through the smallest wire mesh on the gates and pass under the lowest wooden rails in the sheep corrals. When different owners' sheep got mixed together everyone got hot under the collar. Many a dispute was had with other truck drivers and owners over which mouse-sized lamb was his or theirs. I stayed out of the arguments and kept the lambs moving along until they eventually arrived at the ramp where the truck was parked. Once safely loaded we could make the homeward journey, tired but happy. If any sheep had long wool on their bodies Allen would often shear the wool off himself.

Shearing was usually a full day's job. Sometimes it took quite a few days, with all three of us doing the work. I would catch the lambs in the holding pen and take them out to Allen, who was doing the shearing. May looked after the shorn fleeces. She threw the fleece onto the wool table, where she removed any stained wool to put into a separate pile. The fleece was then rolled up and placed into an open wool pack. Wool packs looked like oversized hessian or polyester garbage bags. They sat in a large metal frame that was used to compress all the fleeces tightly to make up a wool bale. When the wool pack could not hold any more fleeces a metal lid was placed on top of the frame and it was squashed down on top of the fleeces using a ratchet cog arrangement attached to the sides. Once it was fully compressed the wool pack full of fleeces was fastened shut. The frame would then be opened so that the bale of wool could be removed. It was now ready to sell.

Allen and I would take the wool bale to the wool store on the way to Newmarket for the next Tuesday sale day. I found the wool store building fascinating. A huge red brick edifice located just north of Melbourne city, it was a remnant of a bygone Australian era that was earmarked for closure, just like the sale yards and abattoir complex. We drove the truck into the building to unload the wool bale, where it would be winched up to the sale floor. While Allen negotiated the sale price I explored the building. It was huge; there was an enormous open bale storage area with a sale floor above overlooking the storage floor. The whole building had timber floors and massive wooden beams holding up the roof and floor levels. I looked at all the timber that was thickly coated in lanolin from the wool and thought that if ever the place caught on fire it would burn with an unbelievable ferocity.

The sale floor was interesting; there were rows upon rows of elevated wooden bins similar to the fruit and vegetable bins in a supermarket. Each held samples of wool that had been taken from the bales stored below. The rows of bins were organized by the quality of the wool contained within them. The finest wools were grouped together. The further one walked away from that area the coarser the quality of the wool. At the other end of the room was the section holding the carpet wool varieties.

When their wool bale was lifted to the storage floor a wool classer slashed holes in the wool pack to pull out samples of the wool contained within. As Allen's wool came from many different breeds of sheep, he was always paid the value of the lowest quality of wool in the bale. To get paid a better price the wool with similar qualities had to be baled together. May decided she would learn wool classing and sort their wool appropriately so that they would be paid a better price. She enrolled in an owner wool classing course at Warragul TAFE. Allen thought it was a stupid idea but she was keen to do it. The classes were held in the evenings and she was nervous about going on the first night, so I went with her. We found the introduction very interesting. May continued attending the course, which took her six months to complete. She told Allen and me many interesting facts about sheep breeds and the wool that they grew. I used the knowledge when we went to the sale yards looking at sheep to buy. Despite this we still ended up buying the cheapest sheep, whatever the type wool they grew on their bodies.

Once she had her certificate and was qualified to class their wool, the sorting of the wool at shearing time changed. The different grades of wool were stored together, with the different types of wool pushed into small sacks. Each sack was labelled with the quality and type of wool that it contained, such as AA fine wool for wool that was shorn from merino type sheep. The bulk of the fleeces were baled with similar fleeces placed in together so that they formed similar wool quality layers in the bale. When it was time to sell the wool the Kensington wool store had closed so we drove to a place in Korumburra where the proprietor took one look at the many sacks and shook his head. "I suppose someone has done an owner wool classing course!" he stated. "It's always the same after someone does a course. What am I supposed to do with all of those small sacks of wool?" The wool sacks were weighed as one lot, then, he took them over to one side of the room, where there were already many small piles of wool. He tipped the contents of the sacks out onto the floor. "It is not much good to me sorted like that I have to re-class it all and keep it until I get some more similar wool that I can bale with it," he told us. "Don't bother sorting it into small lots like that in the future; just bale it all in together, I class all the wool that I buy. Take your empty sacks home with you. I don't want to have to throw them away." We were paid exactly the same price as we got for the previous year's wool that had not been sorted into similar lots. It was fortunate that May enjoyed doing her course, although she was most disappointed that the wool buyer was not complimentary on her classing technique!

After we arrived home on a sale day the animals we bought were settled into paddocks and we would have a late lunch with May before she left to go to her house in Brighton for the night. Lunch times on the farm were special when the three of us related the events of our various activities and the people we interacted with. May would talk about her Brighton neighbours and what Beryl and Wayne were doing if they had been to see her the night before. I talked about my son and his activities and gossip about their friends and parents. May told me things about her childhood and it seemed to me that issues in life appear to be the same throughout the generations. She complained about the school uniform she had as a child. Every time she got a new one – it was always too large - she was told she would grow into it. By the time she had, it was worn out and she had to get a new one – too large, again! I thought nothing has changed with school uniforms; it is still the same today. She also talked about how remote the place she grew up in seemed when she was small, and now it is totally suburban. The same thing is happening where I now live. The cycle of life is repeated throughout the generations.

We all talked about the topical things on the news and the things that were happening in the moment. May liked hearing about our day at the sale yards and the anecdotes about the potential bargain buys that we missed out on or the characters that regularly attended the sales. The thing that struck me as unusual when we were eating was the amount of salt that she ate on her food. At one time when she made some mince, I found the salty taste was so strong that it seemed to take the skin off my tongue. May, however, ate it without a problem although she often complained of getting severe leg cramps at night, saying that it was because she lacked salt. She certainly made up for it in her diet! The very nice soup she made always tasted very salty to me. Despite this she would grab an extra handful of salt to add to her bowl of soup where it would form a small mountain for a few minutes before it dissolved. I wondered how she could eat it. Lovely cakes were also cooked by her, and Allen really enjoyed them. Although the eater had to watch out for the odd cat hair, the cakes still tasted delicious! We would end the meal by doing the dishes together (There was no electric dishwasher in that farmhouse). Then we all headed off in different directions; May to her home in Brighton; Allen to his special friend Mabel's house and me to my son's school to pick him up.

6. May has a Bung Ticker

It is possible that May knew she was sick way before she was diagnosed and worked away on both Allen and I in a silent match making campaign, hoping he would have someone she liked to take care of him when she died. She often encouraged the two of us to go away together. Allen constantly nagged May about everything and I thought maybe she wanted a break from him and his nagging. He never picked at me; he seemed to think that everything I did was perfect. Sometimes we went away with my son. If he was staying with his grandparents or father, the two of us would go off together. May would say, "You two can go away for a few days. I don't want to go anywhere. I'm happy to stay here and look after things." We went to many places around Victoria and New South Wales.

He wanted to take me to Las Vegas in the USA but May became sick and he could not leave her. He told me about a previous trip he had taken with his friend Mabel and what a fabulous time they had in that gambling fantasyland. He sheepishly told me that he was technically a bigamist as they got married in one of the cute little wedding chapels over there but they only went through the ceremony and did not officially register the union. May often referred to Mabel as Alan's special friend. The relationship puzzled me and as I found out it also puzzled their neighbours. May spent nights at her Brighton home and Mabel would come and stay with him in his house at the farm.

Their neighbour who lived opposite told me about when they first bought the farm he saw the evening visitor. He stated that He asked Alan, "Does your wife know about this woman coming to stay with you in the farmhouse?" Alan told him, "Yes." And added as an afterthought, "But perhaps not how often." Allen always explained their married situation as "May believes that sex has only one purpose." "To make babies!" "if you are not planning to make a baby then she believed that there is no reason for us to have sex." He stated that after Beryl was born May told him that she didn't think that she could do that with him anymore, so he respected her wishes and they never had sex again. Their neighbour explained the situation thus: 'What does a man do when he has a high libido and his wife has absolutely no interest in sex? What does a wife do when she finds the prospect of having sex with her husband absolutely repugnant? The sensible thing would be for the wife to try to have more sex with her husband and the husband live on less sex, or they could separate. What if the couple were of the generation that did not readily divorce? If they did not want to separate they could come up with another solution like introduce a third person into their lives. Three homes three people and an interesting solution to an enduring marital problem.

Alan and Mabel regularly went away on holidays together leaving May in charge of the farms etc. The relationship soured when Beryl was getting married because Al was given an ultimatum to divorce May and marry her now that he didn't have a dependent child to consider. Alan did not want to do this as he and May did not want to divide their assets so he ended the relationship.

As it turned out we never went away overseas together, because soon after May died, he developed his own health problems and could not travel long distances.

Allen and May rarely visited the doctors, relying on just getting better naturally when they got sick. In addition to her leg cramping issues, she also had the problem of running out of breath when she exerted herself. This was not thought to have been of any more consequence than the effect of becoming older. She was in her fifties at the time. Unfortunately for her, it was a sign of a more serious underlying health issue that was not diagnosed until 'the dog incident.' On the farm, there were many foxes that caused a problem when the ewes were giving birth. The foxes were very quick to dine on the delightful fresh lamb. It was a battle to keep the lambs alive from birth to about two weeks of age, when they became smart and strong enough to evade them. In the mornings Allen would take a walk out on the property checking on his ewes and lambs.

When he came inside he would give the latest tally of Foxes versus Ewes. "Today it is foxes two, me twenty." To cut down on the fox population he would, from time to time, put out poison baits. He had a dog that was very fond of eating anything that she could find, including fox baits, so she had to be kept tied up or only walked while she was being watched when there were baits around. On one day, after Allen and I had been at his flats to do the gardening and general caretaking, we met May at the farm front gate as we arrived home. She was driving out from the farm and I could see that she was in a very distressed state; something was not right with her. Her face was completely red and her cheeks were puffed up. She explained that the dog had eaten fox bait and she was taking it to the vet. When she returned home later that afternoon, she said that her heart was racing. We all put it down to the stress of the trying to keep the dog alive. The dog recovered but May was not very well. In pain all night, she complained that her left shoulder ached. She could not lie in bed and had to sit up in a chair to sleep. When she eventually went to see a doctor, she was diagnosed with congestive heart failure.

There was a damaged valve in her heart so it could not efficiently pump the blood throughout her body. She blamed the dog for her illness but medical opinion suggested that the problem had existed for a very long time and it was most likely caused by her having Pneumonia or Rheumatic Fever when she was younger. Often people with this type of heart problem could have surgery and an artificial heart valve implanted, but her problem had been in existence for too long and her heart was too enlarged. Surgery was considered unsuitable.

May went onto medication to help her heart function. Allen commented to me that they never believed in taking pills for anything and they laughed at people who did, but now that May was sick she religiously took her prescribed medication as directed. Despite the pills her health deteriorated quite rapidly. She was no longer able to do anything on the farm, and Allen relied heavily on me to assist him. A sad fact was that her specialist told her a heart transplant would save her life but she was too old to be considered as a candidate. Only in her late fifties she still had many more years of life left, although at this time heart transplant surgery was a new medical breakthrough. Surgeons didn't want to risk bad publicity from surgery deaths. Younger people may have seemed a better choice for survivability from the surgery. People far older than that can get transplant surgery now. It seems that only very young people were considered worth saving back then.

7. May is Dying

Two and a half years after May was diagnosed with heart failure her health deteriorated rapidly. She stopped driving to her Brighton home and instead gave it to her daughter to live in with her husband Wayne. It was at about this time that Beryl started keeping company with a male colleague of hers. She brought him down to the farm to stay on weekends and took him horse riding. Allen and May talked about the association but both said that they were not making any comment and decided to not get involved. Wayne, for his part, suddenly 'out of the blue' paid a visit to me one evening. It was a weekend when my son was staying with his father, and as May was now living with Allen in the house at the farm over the road, he knew that it would be unlikely that Allen would be having tea with me as he did in the past when May was at Brighton. He must have presumed that I would be alone. I heard a knock on my front door. It was just becoming dark. When I opened the door there was Wayne, smiling at me. "G'day. How are you going? Can I come in?" His voice was low and husky; I was floored because he was about the last person that I expected to have calling on me. "Allen is not here," I said to him. "I've come to see you," he whispered conspiratorially. I let him into the house and sat him on a chair in the lounge room. Although I felt very awkward in the situation I offered to make him a cup of tea and he accepted. I walked into the kitchen on the pretext of making tea. Allen, being an economical man, had an arrangement with me for when we wanted to contact each other between the two properties. Making a phone call that we answered would cost money so he had a system of ring codes to pass on messages. If I dialled his number and let the phone ring three times and then hung up the phone, it meant that I wanted him to come over to my house. I knew he would be inside the house over the road, as it was night time, so while I was in the kitchen making the tea, I contacted him using the three-ring system without Wayne knowing. Within a couple of minutes Allen walked in the door. It was an embarrassing situation for Wayne. "I'm here, Catherine. What do you ...? WAYNE! WHAT ARE YOU DOING HERE?" Wayne looked very sheepish as he had not expected his father-in-law to walk in the door. "I've come to see you," Wayne replied. "You could see that I wasn't here," declared Allen. They both left and went to the house on the other farm together. Allen never forgot that visit and he often stated that Wayne was sneaky and he didn't like sneaks.

I doubt that Wayne had any feelings for me. I thought that his intention was to use me as a way of taking revenge on his wife and her family or possibly to befriend me and try to find out about this man Beryl had been hanging around. Apart from saying, "Hello" and "How are you" I never paid much attention to him whenever he visited Allen and May. He was always the one who initiated conversations with me. After his visit, Allen felt even stronger feelings of animosity toward him.

By the end of 1988 May was experiencing a rapid decline in her health. She became very disinclined to see her son-in-law and she often complained to Allen when Beryl rang and said that she was coming to visit. "I really don't feel up to having a visit from her. I wish she wouldn't come," she would say to us. On one occasion, a few weeks before she died, May was in the car with Allen and me driving around the farm. When he got out of the car to open a farm gate she confided in me, "I don't feel that I have a daughter anymore. I don't feel that anyone cares whether I live or die. Beryl and Wayne are a pair of greedy vultures waiting for me to die so they can pick my bones clean!" I was flabbergasted and did not know what to say in response. May and her daughter had always had a very close relationship I thought. All I could think to say was, "But you have your sister; isn't she a good friend to you?" May replied, "Oh! She has her own family to care for her; she is too busy to worry about me." I felt very sad when I heard this and said, "I don't want you to die, you are a wonderful friend." Her reply was, "Oh well! It is going to happen and sooner than you think, I would say." She talked about her latest visit to the doctor's, where he discussed how she would die. According to her, the doctor had said it would be peaceful and painless. A blood vessel would burst in her brain and she would have a stroke and then simply and quietly go to sleep forever. I felt troubled. I did not want the status quo to change. Although I liked having Allen organising my life for me, I also liked the freedom to do things I enjoyed doing in the times that he was with

May. Sometimes I liked having my space and free time without him. At times, he could be very controlling.

It was January 1989 and Allen repeatedly told me that May was in a very bad way and he thought that she would die any day. Beryl went overseas to the USA to attend a conference for her work and, as she usually did, included a long holiday in her conference trip. This time she was going to tour South America after the conference. She had only been gone for a few days when her mother died. I remember the day and the doctor very clearly. It was midsummer and the weather was unbelievably hot. Day after day the temperature reached 40 plus degrees Celsius. The hot weather had been causing May a lot of stress. I gave Allen an evaporative cooler that my ex-husband had given to me to help keep her cool. I also suggested to her that she should spend the extremely hot days at my house because I had an air conditioner in my lounge room. It wasn't a particularly good air conditioner; I had bought it cheaply as fire-damaged stock sold off after a local electrical appliance shop had caught on fire. Still, it cooled the house down to a more comfortable level of heat.

May told me that the air cooler was doing an acceptable job cooling her down and she felt happier in her own house. She didn't feel up to moving around from house to house. I did not think that she was doing very well in the heat and I tried to talk Allen into buying a suitable air conditioner. I drove him to a local electrical appliance store and we priced air conditioners. He refused to buy one. "In a couple of days, it will be cold again and I won't need it for another year. I can't see the point in wasting money on something that I will only use a few days a year," he said. I could not understand his frugality as he could afford to buy one and had plenty of money in the bank. He did not seem to consider his wife's needs.

On the fourth day of high temperatures Allen left May sitting in a chair and went out to check that the cows had plenty of water around the farm. He returned to see how May was and shortly after he telephoned me and told me to come over to his house straight away because his wife had died. When I arrived, I saw her seated peacefully in a lounge chair with her feet resting on a small foot stool. Her head was a little to one side instead of upright, and she looked like she was asleep. Allen was tapping her on her shoulder and saying, "May, wake up. Can you wake up?" It was obvious that she was no longer with us so I rang her doctor. It was a Sunday and I got a substitute doctor, who told me that May's regular doctor was away and could not be contacted. He was extremely reluctant about coming out to see her and he kept saying that it was not for him to come out, as the coroner had to come out and check her. I said, "Ok, how do I ring the coroner?" He told me that I couldn't ring the coroner; it was a doctor's job to do that, he had to do it! I asked him to do it and he replied, "No, I have to see the patient first before I can ring the coroner." I said to him, "Then come and see her." He said, "No I can't do that, I am not her doctor" and so the back and forth exchange continued. Oh! The frustration of it was so draining.

This circular discussion went on for about twenty minutes until I suggested that Allen and I would put May in the car and take her to a hospital. This spurred the doctor into saying that he would come out to the house. When he arrived, he was not very sympathetic. I realized that May was dead, but I was rather stunned when the doctor walked up to her and repeatedly jabbed her in her stomach quite vigorously, making it wobble madly, and stated, "Ah yes! Congestive Heart Failure. Her stomach is full of fluid." Apart from briefly listening to her heart through a stethoscope to check that it was no longer ticking, the stomach jabbing was the full extent of his examination. It was obvious to me that her dying had ruined HIS Sunday!

I then had to get the undertaker to take her away so I rang him. Allen insisted that I help him to make the arrangements for the funeral. I felt very uncomfortable doing this, as I was not sure what Beryl wanted, but as she was not around it was up to us. The funeral man was a lovely, sympathetic person. I asked him if they had a freezer to put May in for a week or so, as her daughter was overseas on a holiday. He assured me that they could keep her body refrigerated until a funeral date was set. We had to select a coffin and flowers and decide on the type of ceremony. With Allen's frugality in mind, I did my best to make selections that were in the medium price range. I had to look in

May's wardrobe and find an outfit to give the undertaker for her internment. Meanwhile, the undertaker's assistant wrapped her body in a shroud and placed her on a trolley. He wheeled her out to the hearse, and that was the last time that I ever saw her. After she had gone Allen started rummaging through her personal effects in her handbag. He found a tattslotto ticket for the next week. He never bought tattslotto tickets but he was quite excited about having a free one and made a point of watching the next tattslotto number draw in case he had the winning ticket. I secretly thought that May's spirit could help the desired little numbered balls drop down from the barrel. He did not win anything! Her spirit had let him down. He also found a letter from a lawyer at the bottom of her handbag.

The letter, written some months earlier, was addressed to Wayne Bilk, and outlined the lawyer's concerns over Wayne's correspondence regarding his mother-in-law's estate. It pointed out that Wayne was not concerned for his own welfare but was making the enquiry expressing concerns on behalf of his wife, and made suggestions as to ways in which May could transfer her property to her daughter. Allen was furious about the letter. He felt disgusted by the idea that they had put May under such pressure, particularly as Beryl had often been assured by her mother that she would get her entire assets after she died.

He rang his son-in-law and told him about May dying. Wayne flew over to America and brought Beryl home. She then took over the funeral arrangements and set a date of her choosing. Conveniently for Beryl, I could not attend the funeral because I had to attend an exam for my university postgraduate degree on that day and it could not be changed. The funeral date was not going to be changed for my benefit so I reluctantly went to my exam instead. In hindsight, I wish I had decided on the funeral date while the undertaker was at the house, I was not thinking rationally at the time, I had just lost my friend.

8. Life after May

After the funeral Beryl went to May's lawyer in Dandenong to get her Will. Allen said that her first comment to him was, "I've got the lot!" Her initial thoughts were that she was receiving all her mother's assets, which to her thinking meant that she received half (what she considered her mother's share) of her father's properties. She later found out that she only received the things that her mother owned outright. The jointly owned property, which was the property where I lived, became her father's. All other real estate was solely in her father's name and he retained ownership of it all. Allen kept telling his daughter that she had been given a damn good serve and was well looked after but she continually complained that she wasn't given enough.

Her mother's estate included the Brighton home where she and her husband lived, her shares in the family button wholesaling company (including the shares that Allen had paid for), her cash in her bank account and the vast quantity of antiques and paintings within the house. On her probate documents, she valued the estate at $780,000. The house alone was worth much more than the valuation on the probate documentation, as neighbouring properties were being sold for the value of the land at over a million dollars and her property included two blocks. The house was built on one block and another was used for the tennis court. In current day values, it would be equal to four or five million. She was the typical 'poor little rich girl.' Soon after her mother's death, Allen informed me that Beryl was offered two million dollars by someone who wanted to buy her house. She said that the offer was not enough, and that the house was worth much more than that and continued to complain to her father that she wasn't given enough in her mother's estate.

May left Allen with another major problem. At the time of her death she had about a hundred or so cats. Unfortunately, they had to have the Egyptian King treatment and join her in the afterlife. Most were either, too diseased, too old or too wild to be given to anyone. I had no idea how we could catch them anyway. The cats only knew May, but even she could not touch many of them. Allen decided to shoot them. I was at work when the assassinations happened, I did not want to be around anyway. The poor cats were sitting ducks to Allen and his rifle. He put out food for them and while they were eating he aimed and fired, and, although the cats were very nervous and jumpy about the shooting, their hunger was too great so they stayed eating while the carnage happened around them. The good thing was that he was a very accurate shot, so death was instantaneous.

I begged him to spare the friendly ones that I liked and I was very disappointed that they copped it as well. He told me that he mistook which ones were the friendly ones and which ones were the wild ones. It took him a couple of weeks to eliminate every cat. In total, he shot ninety seven cats. I thought there were more than that, I presume that some managed to run away and live somewhere else.

Allen wanted to sell his farms after the death of his wife. At the time, his undiagnosed Parkinson's symptoms were affecting him. He approached a local Real Estate agent and had valuations made on the two properties. The agent prepared and printed sale brochures. One farm was valued at eight- hundred thousand dollars, the other, because it had better improvements, one million dollars. Beryl, however, did not want him to sell any properties. She would tell him, "Now is not a good time to sell." She often criticized him for all the properties that he had sold in the past and how much they would be worth if he still had them. She would say to him, "You have always been a seller. You could have been very rich if you hadn't kept selling everything. Some of the properties that you owned are worth millions now!" Allen told me that he loved me and asked me if I wanted to stay and help him with his farms if he didn't sell them. He decided that he couldn't continue without my help and he didn't want to give the farms to Beryl as they were his life achievement. We agreed that we really enjoyed being together and wanted to continue living with each other as a couple. I told him that I loved him and being with him was all that I wanted from life. He cancelled the property sale arrangements that had been made, when we started living together. We also discussed getting married but it never eventuated.

From the time we started living together after May had died, I spent the next eighteen years of my life helping Allen maintain and retain all his properties that he still owned. This is something that he could not have done without my help. During that time, the value of the properties increased dramatically due to the increasing urbanization of the surrounding suburbs. He could have leased the farms, and not have to do any more work on them. He had many people ask him if he would do so, but he did not want to do that as he did not like anyone telling him what to do with his things. He did not want anyone in control of his assets, and wanted to be the sole boss, which is why he wanted me to help him. He was happy because he could control me. He could have given property to his daughter but would say, "I don't want them coming down ordering me around and making decisions without asking me." He felt that his daughter should not expect it to be her automatic right to have his assets, especially as she had already been given his matrimonial home when her mother died. He would often say, "Beryl has already been well looked after." In the years after May's death he would be quite angry that Beryl was given his wife's house outright.

Considering all the years that he had paid the bills and maintained the house, he felt that he should have been given half or at the least a life interest in the house. I often had discussions with him.

Me: "Why do you want the house? Do you want to live there?"

Allen: "No."

Me: *"If you had the house, what would you do with it?"*

Allen: "I would probably sell it."

Me: *"What would you do with the money? Would you spend it?"*

Allen: "I don't know. Put it in the bank, I suppose."

Me: *"You don't spend the money that you already have. You really don't need any more so they might as well have the house. Don't you think?"*

Allen: "I guess so but I still should have been given something for all the years that I paid the rates."

He was thinking back to the years that the Brighton house was their main family residence when he paid all the rates, insurance and maintenance costs until it was given to Beryl along with the family company shares that he had paid for all those years ago. He was very peeved about that and would say, "The shares are not worth as much as they were in the past. Wayne is not as clever as he thinks himself to be. His advice is always wrong." Sometimes Allen had trouble getting over things, and he tended to hold grudges forever and was always commenting that the contents of the Brighton house would be worth hundreds of thousands of dollars. Many of the items had been handed down through the generations, and others had been bought by Beryl's grandfather during his travels overseas. There were paintings, antique furniture and various antiquities such as a full suit of knight's armour.

There was a lot of friction between father and daughter during the time shortly after May's death. On the weekends, she would visit him at the farm and clean the house for him. He would complain bitterly that as she was cleaning the house she was filling her car with items from his house and taking them to her own home, although he was never asked whether she could take anything. To add insult to injury, Beryl had Allen under strict instructions that he was not allowed to sell anything in his own house on the farm, as she wanted it all. This got under his skin and he tended to be in a very bad mood after her visits.

To spite his daughter, he began surreptitiously selling items in his house. An avid reader of the newspapers, he would read the auction advertisements and on many occasions, he would read out to me the details about particular specialist antique auctions that were advertised. As he had antique items in his house similar to what was being sold, he would decide to sell his own. In one newspaper, he read an advertisement about an impending auction sale of antique guns and became very excited. He said that May had an antique gun somewhere in the house and made me help him search for it, but I didn't have a clue where to look. Allen said, "I know where to look. It will be under her bed." When she was alive May slept on a wooden-based bed that had storage drawers in the base. He looked in the drawers but there was no gun. It wasn't under the mattress either. Then he pulled the drawers out completely and there, hidden in the frame, was the gun! He said, "You just have to know people. I knew it would be somewhere here. I knew she would keep it close to where she was sleeping." He took it to the auctioneer's building and offered it for sale. It was a very ornate flintlock pistol that turned out to be of Afghani or Persian origin from early in the 20th century and he was paid $600 dollars for it.

He regularly sold off little items like this whenever he got peeved with his daughter. This little subterfuge gave him a feeling of delight, a sort of one-upmanship or power over her. I was never allowed to tell her about his little clandestine sales. Even worse than that, after the birth of Beryl's first child Allen would drive to her Brighton home on one day each week to mind the baby so that she could go shopping. He would ring me while he was there for baby care advice as the baby would be crying and he could not placate it. I was not much more experienced than him at baby care, so it was a case of the 'blind leading the blind' in this situation.

In addition to child minding, he had his own agenda: while he was at the house he would take antique items and bring them back to the farm with him. In the evening when I got home from work he would have his latest treasure there to show me. I just stayed out of the whole business. It had nothing to do with me, so I turned a blind eye to his activities. He would often say, "Beryl has so much stuff in that house that she wouldn't know what she has." Eventually he sold the things that he had taken. I doubt that she ever realized what he had been doing right under her nose.

For about ten years after May's death Allen and I enjoyed our blissful life together. I remember watching a scene in movie on TV called 'The Ballad of Cable Hogue' where a couple lived an idyllic life running a stage coach rest stop in the American desert. The story was set some time in the past. While the woman sang a song, 'Butterfly Mornings and Wildflower Afternoons' there were scenes of the two of them doing chores together and enjoying each other's companionship.

I thought this perfectly described our life together. Not opulent or extravagant just simple, cosy and happy. At night when we went to bed we revelled in telling each other about the things that happened during our day. We especially liked talking about the funnier things. People have many different life experiences and different personalities and in most places of employment a variety of personality types make up the staff. The education system has its fair share of unique personalities. After I started working as a teacher I met quite a few characters at my work. Some were teacher colleagues and others were the students. At night, I delighted Allen with little anecdotes about my day. If my day was not interesting enough, I would exaggerate my reiteration a little to make him laugh. My students were the most interesting, as they came from many different countries and their stories about their earlier lives were most illuminating. Many had sad stories about their former countries but overall, they were grateful for the opportunity to come to Australia to live. Allen enjoyed hearing about my students' lives. His comment always was, "We really do live in a lucky country."

9. Early Signs of Ill Health

In hindsight, it is apparent that Allen was experiencing early symptoms of Parkinson's disease, the disease that shortened his life, in 1979/1980. He often complained to May and me that he was not very well. He thought that he was going to die soon. He would say, "How are you going to manage without me?" May would reply, "First I would sell all of the sheep, as looking after them is too much hard work. But you are not going to die. Creaky gates always last longest." Back then he exhibited many of the now-known early signs. At the time, no one connected the symptoms with any serious disease. The Parkinson's indicators were there but they did not have any big effect on his day-to-day living; they were merely considered to be a consequence of him becoming older.

One of the earliest signs of Parkinson's disease is the loss of the sense of smell. At the time that I first knew Allen he had already lost his sense of smell. Unbeknown to anyone around him, this was the forerunner of him developing more serious Parkinson's symptoms. He had a dog that was always passing wind when travelling in vehicles. Whenever May or I were in the car with them we had to have the window open to disperse the odour. I found myself gagging on the stench from the dog but Allen could smell nothing. With his veritable sense of humour, he would comment that he was receiving the nourishment from the dog's flatulence but not the aroma. His sense of humour was exceptional, particularly when it came to flatulence. Although he was a gentleman in the truest sense he still had his raunchy, funny side. As the Eskimos have many different words to describe snow, he had his own vernacular to describe flatulence: puffballs, bubbles and gravy were a few of them. One needs to use his/her own imagination to work out which types of wind would equate with each particular nomenclature.

Another early Parkinson symptom is vivid dreaming. Allen regularly had very vivid, active dreams and was prone to screaming out at night when having them. He would even jump out of bed, run around the bedroom and start punching the walls, attempting to defend himself from his dreamland attackers. May and I often laughed with him when he recounted his dreams to us. As they slept in separate bedrooms, his wife often missed his night time antics. It was some years later when I was reading literature about Parkinson's disease that I found out about vivid dreams being an early symptom.

Thinking back, I realized that I often may have been the victim of Allen's vivid dreams after we started living together and sharing a bed. Many times, I would get up in the mornings feeling a little sore and bruised in places. I never associated it with his dreaming - he told me I often would stir in my sleep when he was restless and grab his hands and talk soothingly to him to settle him down, although I was never aware that I was doing this, as I am a very sound sleeper.

Allen lost his sense of balance. It first became apparent when he developed a problem with climbing on ladders. He could not handle heights without becoming dizzy and losing his balance. He was able to climb ladders when I first knew him but as time passed he seemed to not be able to do it anymore. I had to do all the high work for him. There was a lot of ladder climbing work to do as he liked to do most of the caretaking jobs on the blocks of flats that he owned. After May started having her own health issues I would usually go with him to help with his weekly property maintenance trips. I had to climb up trees to trim the tops off from over the roofline and clear out the leaves from the gutters on his double story block of flats. He would get quotes from trades-people to get these jobs, but he always felt that the price was too high and he could do it himself! The "himself" usually ended up being me.

As time passed his sense of balance steadily deteriorated. In the early part of our relationship he could stand on one foot to put on a sock when he was dressing. A few years later he lost this ability. He would get up out of bed in the morning and try to put on his socks while standing up. He could not do it! I found it very funny watching him hopping all around the room on one foot trying to keep his balance after he lifted his other foot to put on his sock. He would have the sock dangling from his hands and one foot cocked up in the air, desperately trying to get it over his toes before he fell. Eventually he would fall onto the bed. I would tell him, "Why don't you sit on the bed to put on your socks?" It would make his life easier if he did that but for some reason he always tried to do it from a standing position. He did not have a problem with putting on his shoes or trousers; it was only his socks. Neither of us thought that his balance problem was anything to worry about. He was getting older and we thought it was a problem associated with his age and not caused by any medical condition.

Even more interesting was watching him trying to undo cellophane wrapping on things. Cheese slices that were individually wrapped posed a major problem for him. At the time, I thought it was his eyesight that was going bad as he couldn't see the end of the wrapper, but it was in fact his fine motor skills needed for manipulating objects that were failing him. Lastly, he had night time attacks of shivering and shaking while sweating profusely. It was this last symptom which led to us living together as a couple, as by this time May had died and I was divorced. I was living in a house that I had bought about a kilometre away from Allen's farms. After his wife's death, he continued living on their farm. Every couple of months he would ring me in the middle of the night, telling me that he was dying and asking me to come to his house to help him call an ambulance.

When I arrived, he was usually in a very bad state, dripping wet from perspiration while shivering violently. These attacks would last for about thirty to forty minutes. By the time I arrived his shuddering attacks would have eased somewhat but he would still be wet and shivery. He would say, "I am not so bad now. Let's just wait for a bit to see if I get better." I would sit with him and offer comfort during these attacks. We talked about his symptoms but I had no suggestions as to what could be wrong. I thought it had something to do with him being a widower and lonely. These attacks happened regularly until after he was diagnosed with Parkinson's disease and started taking medication. The Parkinson's drugs controlled the sweating attacks and they ceased to happen until the final few weeks of his life, when they returned.

During the night time when I went to help him, we chatted and he would tell me that he loved me. He wanted me to sell my house and live with him.

He told me about his real estate deals and promised me that we could buy and sell houses together and make lots of money. He even talked about marriage and having more children with me. I was very young and gullible at the time and believed every word, I grew wiser with age. After we started our relationship Allen, my son and I spent many weekends going to the beach and driving around the beachside suburbs of Black Rock and Beaumaris inspecting houses that were for sale. He wanted us to buy houses in need of renovation so that we could fix them up and resell them for a profit. He always complained about the houses being too expensive as he used to buy similar houses in the area for half the price in earlier years. As he already had a good property portfolio, he became reluctant to venture into buying more property and would say, "I have already done my bit and I am too old to do any more. You should buy places on your own and I will help you."

He convinced me to move back to live in his house with him. I wanted to keep my own house and rent it out, but he was dead against that idea, insisting that I would have problems with tenants and it would be too much stress for me. I was eventually talked into selling my house. As time passed I became convinced that he never had any intention of doing any house buying or renovating with me because he did not want me living away from him and out of his control. Allen was a very controlling man. However, he had a considerate side and if I told him something was very important to me he would consider the matter for a day or two. We would then discuss it again where he would usually agree with my view.

After he became sick I spent most of the school end of term holiday breaks taking him to various medical appointments. If I had been in any other type of job I would have had to give up my work to care for him. I liked having the regular income from my job, as he did not like spending his money. He happily went without while his cash reserves steadily increased. I moved up the pay scale to become a leading teacher. This was a more highly paid position than I would have had on a regular teacher's wage. My income turned out to be very necessary when I had to employ the services of lawyers after his death.

Although he was not always entirely well, Allen was still able to live an almost normal life. We went away camping and regularly went around the Victorian coast, enjoying the fabulous beaches and walking trails that Parks Victoria had made throughout the State. I often booked interstate airfares when they were on sale and we would go away for a few days. He could not bring himself to spend much money on these holiday jaunts, so we ended up spending nights in some rather grim accommodations. The worst place was a very, very, cheap hotel in Sydney. It was some sort of backpacker place or something worse, and it cost only $2.00 per person. Allen loved a bargain! I wasn't one to complain too much but this one took the cake. The place was infested with fleas and I spent the worst night scratching and being uncomfortable. Not one flea bothered him and he was convinced that I was imagining them.

Another extremely grim place where we spent a night was in Wagga Wagga in New South Wales. After he had completed year twelve, my son had joined the Army Reserve and spent twelve months training there. Allen and I went to Wagga Wagga to watch him graduate from his first year of training and to see the army displays and parades. Because of his father's military background Allen had a keen interest in anything to do with the military, so he was very eager to go. We arrived and looked around for accommodation. As we drove past a caravan park he saw a sign advertising the price for a night's stay and decided that it was the price that he wanted to pay, so in we went.

The caravan was quite nice but there was no heating! It was a mild, sunny winter day so it didn't seem too much of a problem. That night the temperature dropped by many degrees. It was freezing! We huddled together for warmth and still we were frozen. I found a toaster in the cupboard. It was a very old fashioned type that had small doors on each side that had to be opened to put in the bread. I turned on the toaster and propped the doors open but even that could not take much of the chill out of the air. The next day Allen decided that he was too old to rough it in a place like that caravan park; it was just too cold. When he was a young man he would have found the caravan quite luxurious compared to some of the army camps that he stayed in during his youth but not anymore. We went to a nice hotel for the rest of our stay in Wagga Wagga. The caravan experience was never repeated; whenever we went away after that he agreed to us staying in reasonable hotels.

Allen also learnt to cook about this time. Before this he always had someone else cook for him and apart from making marmalade, he never thought to try cooking himself. It was something he discovered that he enjoyed doing very much. He cooked basic meals but he really liked learning how to cook different things. The idea first came to him from my work colleagues who we regularly socialized with. One couple often invited us for dinner. The husband did the cooking and was an excellent cook. Allen was so impressed that he decided to try his hand at cooking also. From then on, he cooked the evening meals every night. He became a dab hand at cooking grilled meat and veggies, and he kept boasting that he was soon going to progress to 'roasts'. Unfortunately, his health deteriorated so much that he stopped cooking entirely and soon he forgot that he had ever cooked at all.

10. Allen gets Sick

Allen tended to get up several times in the night to go to the toilet. He was in his late 50s at the time. This seemed to be quite abnormal for a man of his age and he sought medical advice about it, visiting specialists and having x-rays and tests done to see if it was a health issue. It was decided that he could have prostate problems so he visited a Specialist Urologist whose opinion was that he had a slight enlargement of his prostate, however he did not think that it was the reason for his bladder problems. The doctor suggested that surgery was an option but not necessarily essential at that time. Beryl seemed quite adamant that he should have surgery and was pressuring him to have it done right away. According to Allen, she told him that he would find himself unable to go to the toilet at all as he would become blocked up. I kept telling him that the doctor had said surgery wasn't urgent and, as he lived in Australia, not a third world country, if he had a problem with his bladder hospitals and medical help were only minutes away. He could easily get treatment if it became serious. At his daughter's insistence, he decided to go ahead and have the surgery. This was a major mistake and I felt that she was to blame for the rapid decline in his health after the surgery. It did not make one bit of difference to his nocturnal bathroom trips but it brought on the more significant Parkinson's disease symptoms. The operation involved the use of spinal anaesthesia where a needle was inserted into his spine to inject the anaesthetic. Immediately after he woke up from the anaesthetic he was in a bad way. He recovered quickly from the prostate part of the operation but had major problems with his legs and walking, with tremors and shuddering in his muscles. It was concluded that the spinal injection had somehow affected the nerves in his spine. Had he not had the surgery, maybe it would have taken a lot longer for him to develop the more serious Parkinson's problem.

The months immediately after his surgery were hell for Allen. He kept complaining that his legs felt like lumps of wood. He could not drive a car and had to sit down after walking short distances. This was in stark contrast to the way he could stride out for kilometres before his operation. His legs filled with fluid causing his normally slender long legs to look like an elephant's. He was diagnosed as having oedema in his legs caused by being inactive and not walking enough. We had a spinning wheel with a foot treadle that we used on occasions to spin sheep's wool into yarn, and I got him to peddle this while sitting in the lounge watching TV. The activity reduced the leg fluid a little but it was not a cure.

Our life became an endless round of visits to medical specialists, leading to various tests to try to determine what was causing his health problems. Tests were done for cow-borne diseases such as leptospirosis and many other infections, none of which were positive. Another specialist inserted small electrode probes into his leg muscles, which caused the muscles to tremor, and he also had a lot of probing done to his body. I imagined him like a pin cushion with all the needles that were being poked into him. When he drank something, I had cartoon-like visions of the fluid squirting out from all of his needle holes! None of the tests seemed to provide a reason for his health problems and it was usually suggested that his problems were a direct result of the spinal anaesthetic that was used for the prostate operation. The conclusion was that he would eventually get better.

After a few months, he recovered sufficiently to return to an activity level that was somewhat akin to what he was like before the surgery; however, he was not fully healthy. He still needed to get up in the night to go to the toilet so his surgery did not improve that situation at all. In addition, he seemed to be falling over a lot more often. Initially I did not think that his falls were such a big deal as I never saw him falling and I only had his explanation as to why he fell. I recall one specific evening when I arrived home from work and he told me about his falling over in the paddock that day. The way that he described the event made it seem so funny that we laughed about it. It was winter and the mornings were very foggy. The fog was so thick that visibility was down to about two metres. He described the scene to me. "I was walking in the paddock when I tripped on a lump of dirt and fell over. I could not stand up so I had to crawl on my hands and knees along the ground until I could find a fence to grab onto to pull myself up. When I reached the fence, I was able to stand but because the fog was so dense I could not see more than a few metres ahead of me. I could not decide where I was so I spent the next hour aimlessly wandering around in the gloom trying to find my way back to the house."

In the back of my mind I found it hard to believe that he could not work out where he was. In the past he never had any trouble finding his way around the farms on foggy days, even if it was a pitch black night. I felt a sense of apprehension about what was wrong with him but I didn't say anything. The falling episodes continued to happen on a regular basis over the next couple of years. I would arrive home from work to be shocked by the sight of him with blood-covered gashes on his head or body as the result of his latest fall and would listen to his explanation for his mishap. He would tell me things like, "I was climbing through a fence when my trouser leg got caught on the barbed wire and I lost my balance and fell on my head. I got my boot caught in some long grass and tripped. I tried to step over a tree branch when it flicked up and I fell onto it." These incidents started to become more frequent and I was becoming very alarmed. In addition, his legs were still giving him trouble, particularly at night when he was regularly having night-time muscle tremors and sweating sessions. Many doctor's visits ensued until he was finally diagnosed with Parkinson's disease and went under the care of a neurologist, Doctor William Dendrite.

He started taking Parkinson's medication and his leg problems, night sweats and falling incidents were mostly resolved. We were told by Doctor Dendrite that waking up in the night was caused by the disease. Allen's brain would run out of dopamine, a chemical that is necessary for certain brain functions, and he would wake up. He would decide that he awoke because he wanted to go to the toilet and off he would go. The little walk would help raise the dopamine levels in his brain and he would settle back to sleep until the dopamine levels dropped again, and so the nightly cycle continued. He did not even need the prostate surgery! His nightly toilet trips were less frequent when he first started on his medication but he still needed to rise two or three times a night. A habit had been established that he could not break.

Initially his nocturnal activity was not a problem for me as I am a very sound sleeper so was not aware of his getting up throughout the night. As time passed and his motor skills deteriorated, he required my assistance to carry out his nocturnal toilet visits. His night vision became so poor that he needed to turn on a light to walk to the toilet. He had a bedside lamp that turned on with a small pull cord, however he could not pull the cord to turn on the lamp. It seemed incredible to me that the simple act of pulling the lamp cord was unachievable for him. Parkinson's disease affects everyday life in little ways that the average person could not imagine. I solved this problem by buying a touch lamp and rejoiced in the fact that we lived in a technological era where there was a solution for little situations like that. As the years passed his need to rise in the night became more of a problem, due to blood pressure problems. If he got up too quickly his blood pressure would drop suddenly and he would fall to the ground. This was particularly a problem if he tried to rise from a reclining position such as when he was lying in bed, as the blood pressure drop was too great. He had to bring his head and upper torso into a sitting position and wait for a minute before putting his legs over the side of the bed and if he did not do this he would suddenly fall back to a supine position. If he was lucky this would be back on the bed, otherwise it was a disaster.

11. Life with a Parkinson's Person

In the first few years following the initial Parkinson's diagnosis his life did not change very much. His medication worked sufficiently to allow him to be as active as he had been before his prostate surgery although he hated taking his medication. In fact, he did not like taking medication of any type, not even headache tablets, so he was extremely annoyed at having to take so many tablets throughout the day on a daily basis. Amazingly, he seemed to forget all of his health problems that he had been having before he started taking his medication. I tried to remind him of what he was like before and that the pills were making his current lifestyle possible but he did not agree. He joined a Parkinson's support group which met monthly. The group was attended by Parkinson's sufferers, accompanied by a bevy of relatives. I was impressed by the way so many families would rally to help a sick relative. The daughters of many of the Parkinson's sufferers attended with their parents to learn the latest news on care and treatment ideas. I felt that their commitment was admirable, with them caring for a sick parent while simultaneously juggling work commitments and child rearing duties.

Meeting with lots of other Parkinson's sufferers was very useful because we could discuss the treatments that each person had tried and found helpful, and which treatments were not successful. We could compare symptoms for the disease itself and the side effects of the various medications that were available. In addition, there were trained professionals who gave us advice on health issues specifically related to the disease and ways to manage it that would improve Allen's quality of life. I referred to these meetings as going to creaky club, and this was the terminology that he embraced in private when we talked about it. In the early stages of the disease when he was still quite active, he would listen to others talk about taking their pills on time and he would have a private laugh about it. One man told him, "Taking your pills on time is very important. You need to take your morning pills on time because you need to have a shower and then towel yourself down. This takes a lot of strength away from you. So, you need to have taken your pills so that you can keep going." He thought that this was an exaggeration as he did not find taking a shower tiring. Neither of us realized that this was how he would end up, let alone get far worse.

At creaky club he met another man who did not take any medication at all, declaring that the medication would only work for a certain number of years and then it would fail and then he would be left without any available treatment options. Allen was quite angry about the fact that he was just as well as this man but he was taking medication and this man was not. I could not convince him that he was not living a very satisfactory life before he started taking pills. He kept thinking that he should not be taking tablets and he was stuck taking them because of everyone around him saying that he had to take them. He just did not like taking pills!

I also attended many creaky club meetings with him and they were very informative as the people that we met were in various stages of the disease. We could discuss with other sufferers and their relatives', topics like which pill combinations worked for each person, dosage rate, and could compare the side effects that the different pill combinations had on individual people. The person with the disease seemed to have a different opinion to the person who was caring for him/her. We learnt about the progress of the disease and care requirements. Also, the presenters talked about the various treatment options that could be used when a person's current medication regimen failed to work adequately.

During the mid-stages of his disease I had to make quite a few modifications to the house and its surroundings to make Allen's life more comfortable. He could not turn taps on or off and had to wait for someone to come to his aid whenever he wanted to turn a tap on. I solved this little problem by replacing all the taps in the house with flick mixer taps. These did not require turning on or off just a flip up of the handle for 'on' and down again for 'off'. He managed to turn these taps on and off easily. The bathroom was located centrally in the house but the toilet was at the back. It required him to negotiate a small step to get to it.

He had a major problem with stepping down the ten-centimetre step. I modified the bathroom and installed a toilet in there. Now he did not have to walk so far for his toilet trips and there was no step to contend with. He had major problems with keeping his body warm in winter and cool in summer so I arranged for a split system air conditioning unit to be installed for hot weather and gas heating for winter. This meant that the whole house could be kept at the same temperature. Before this we had a wood fire for heating but it required a lot of work loading wood in throughout the day to keep it burning. Installing the gas heating was quite a major undertaking as the gas main was at the front fence, one hundred and fifty metres away from the house, but I managed to get the job done and we enjoyed the type of comfort that city dwellers take for granted. We had the pleasure of having instant heating at the push of a button.

Allen often tripped when walking on uneven ground surfaces when he was walking around the garden. Originally the house had only lawn surrounding it which was very uneven and became quite slushy in the winter when it rained. I had to have concrete paths made around the house so that he had a smooth surface to walk on. Lights had to be installed outside around the house to illuminate the paths, due to the loss of his night vision. Without lighting, it was very difficult for him to walk from the car that was in a detached garage to the house if it was dark. He hated these home alterations and would not accept that he needed these changes. In his mind, his predicament was only temporary and he would recover so I was wasting money. Gradually he became accustomed to things and forgot that it was any different.

At around this time, in the late 1990s, we were living together permanently and the matrimonial home on the other farm was vacant. It had been vacant since May's death ten years previously. Allen rarely entered the house, as there were three steps to ascend to get into it and he was no longer able to go up or down steps unaided. I would try to help him up the stairs but I was not strong enough to give him the support that he needed. Often, he didn't feel secure enough to go up the steps so he preferred to not go inside. The house had been left untouched since he had stopped living there although all the furnishings and contents remained. One night it was burgled and antiques and paintings were stolen. Some of the paintings were by a renowned Australian First World War artist who knew Allen's parents. Another was painted by H. Septimus Power, another family friend. I did not particularly like this artwork. One of the paintings was huge, about a metre by a metre and a half in size, with an enormous filigree-carved, gilded frame. It depicted a wagon on a country road with fields in the foreground with the background all painted with harsh, dull, olive greens, dirty, mauves and greys. The use of muted, sombre colours did not appeal to me. Even the wagon and fields were painted in sombre shades of brown. I felt that it was a depressing painting but Allen felt depressed about his loss of it.

He thought that the burglars could return and the rest of the house's contents could be stolen. Much of the furniture was antique and came from his grandmother's home and was very old and beautifully made. He decided that he would sell all the house contents before anything else was stolen, and contacted a local antiques dealer who came out and bought most of the furniture. I did not want him to sell the furniture. Whenever I went inside that house after the sale I felt a profound sense of loss. This was partly due to the furniture being gone, the feeling of emptiness left behind and Allen's health problems. I sensed my life with him was coming to an end.

I really missed the early days, his health and the life that we enjoyed together in the past. I would sit on his bed, which had not been sold, reminiscing about the nights when we had slept together in it, and shed a tear or two. The furniture, the trinkets, the fun and the laughter were gone from our life, to be replaced by a bitter, ailing and unhappy man who also missed the fun and good times.

Now that the house was cleared of furniture I suggested that he rent it out. Sitting vacant meant the condition of it was going downhill. Literally, that is! The stumps were rotting away and the floor had definite uphill and downhill sections. To bring it up to a rental standard I got quotes from tradesmen for repairs. As I obtained more quotes for the various work that needed doing, the cost started to rise. The corrugated iron roof was quite rusted and it leaked. The stumps were rotted away. The water pipes which were made of galvanized iron, were very corroded, and also leaked, so the entire plumbing needed to be renewed. The electrical wiring was in a bad way due to possums living in the roof cavity. Sometimes switching on a light would cause the fuses to blow due to shorts in the wiring. The plaster was full of holes due to the leaking roof. The cost was getting close to sixty thousand dollars, and the original old fashioned kitchen and bathroom had not been considered yet. Allen did not want to pay to repair the house, claiming it would be better to put a match to it. I filed all the quotes away in my filing cabinet under 'House Repair Quotes.' The house stayed vacant and became more and more ramshackle as years passed.

12. Allen making Wills

After Allen's death, there were eight Wills in existence. These were made over several years. The seventh was made by his lawyer at the behest of Beryl and Wayne but it was never executed as Allen refused to sign it. The one consistent feature of the first six of the eight wills was the fact that the farm where we had lived together was gifted to me. The Will-making saga began in 1998 when the laws changed for de-facto partners. Prior to this a de-facto partner of someone who died did not have much recourse to sue an estate if he or she was not adequately provided for in the deceased's Will. With the change in the law, de-facto partners had rights similar to those of a wife or husband. It was around about this time that Allen's Parkinson's medication started to become less effective. One night a crashing sound woke me. It was the middle of the night and he was out of bed trying to walk to the toilet. He could not walk properly; his blood pressure had dropped and he was crashing against the walls, the cupboard doors and finally he fell by the bedroom door. I jumped out of bed and ran to help him up and he said to me, "I'm not too good tonight. I am getting worse and I am going to get a whole lot worse, you know." I already knew this. "I need you to stay with me and look after me. I am going to make a will and I am going to give you this farm if you promise to stick around and look after me. Will you do this? Will you look after me until I die?" I assured him that I would stay with him. He said, "I will give you this farm and I will also give you some money and another property. I haven't decided how much money or which other property yet but that is what I will do." He told me that Beryl was insisting that he update his will and he would be going to a lawyer to do this fairly soon. I had to promise to stay with him and look after him.

It seemed to me that the problem with Allen's testamentary intention was to do with his daughter having her own ideas as to how his will should be written and how his assets should be distributed. As his health began to deteriorate and his Parkinson's disease symptoms became more obvious, she often rang to converse with him. He usually confided in me after these conversations that his assets and how his estate was to be distributed after he died were the major focus of the call. They would end up having yelling arguments over the phone. He would be jabbing at his chest with his index finger (not that she could see that), whilst yelling at her, "It's my money, mine, Mine, MINE! I can do what I want with it. I can piss it up against a wall if I want!" She would be yelling back at him and he would end the argument by hanging up on her, loudly slamming down the phone receiver. He would be in a bad mood for days. Beryl would usually ring and apologize a week or two later, but often she wouldn't because they only ended up arguing again.

If I was home when she came to the farm to visit, she would take him for a walk outside or put him in his car and take him for a drive around the farms. I always felt shut out. I knew that she wanted to discuss his assets with him away from me. She did not consider that I had any rights or the fact that he still owned the assets that had increased most in value, his farms, because of me helping him. When they returned she would not say goodbye to me. She would get straight into her car and zoom off down the drive. Her father would come into the house in a volatile mood, ranting and raving about his money and how everyone was greedy and only after his money. The visits from her always seemed to end in an argument between them, often leading him to decide that he would be better off on his own. He wanted to move out of the house we lived in and back to the house on the other farm. I would watch him pack his kit and sometimes help him, but I never made any comment. There was no point. He would make himself a sandwich, pack a few tea bags and put some milk in a jam jar. Then off he would go in his car. I would busy myself around the house, cleaning, doing something that needed doing or simply enjoy a little solitude. After a few hours, when it started to get dark, I would cook dinner, for two of course. It was time to rescue Allen!

Over the road to the other house I would drive. There, he would be sitting in the only chair left. It was the one chair that the antique dealer who bought the other household furniture considered not suitable to resell as an antique. He would be in the lounge room watching the news on his ancient TV, looking as miserable as all heck. In I would go, sit on his lap, cuddle up to him and ask him how he was feeling. "I'm cold and lonely." (If it was winter) "I'm too hot and lonely." (If it was summer) "I was hoping you would come. I'm starving and I only have a sandwich; is there anything to eat at home?" I would tell him that his dinner was ready. "Oh!" he would reply, "I was hoping that you had cooked dinner." We would return to the house where we lived together and, although I never questioned him about his arguments with Beryl, after a few days he would often want to talk. The arguments always seemed to involve his money and his involvement with me. There was not much I could do about it so our life continued as usual. Peace reigned until her next visit!

In 1998 Beryl made an appointment with a legal firm in Cranbourne with Mr. Jeff Cranberry of Cranberry Law Pty Ltd and took her father to make a Will. Allen, in keeping with some of his agreement that he made with me, gifted the property where we lived to me and twenty thousand dollars in cash. The rest of his estate that comprised the other farm, about one and a quarter million dollars, two blocks of flats (12 in all) and about sixty-thousand dollars' worth of shares went to his daughter Beryl and her children. Beryl was to be the executor of the estate.

Allen told me later that she made it very clear to the lawyer that I was merely a friend and insisted that the Will be worded as such. He also informed me that she implied to the lawyer that I was not a very nice person and made him out to be an unfortunate and vulnerable person. I asked him why he didn't defend me and he said that she wouldn't let him speak and he didn't want to make a scene by arguing with her at the lawyer's office. There was no way that he could be thought of as vulnerable; he always said his mind and would stand up to anyone. Although he was not a volatile man by nature, when he got hot under the collar he would argue with people and not back down. Whenever he had arguments with his adjoining neighbours over the dividing fences or arguments with other people over the years, he always firmly stood his ground. He did not give in if he felt that he was in the right. He had been a businessman and he would not have been able to achieve what he had in life if he had been a pushover.

After he made that Will, he kept saying that he was giving his daughter too much and I should be getting more, as I would not be able to maintain the farm on my teacher's income. Some months later he went back to the same lawyer and made another Will, still giving me the farm as promised, but added 40% of his money to be given to me as well. Beryl was to get the other farm and she shared the remainder of his assets with her children. He also made the lawyer the executor for his estate. I did not ask him to do this; I was at work it was entirely his own decision. The next day he rang Beryl at her work and told her about the Will change. According to Allen she lost her temper and screamed at him, "My children are not getting enough! You are giving Catherine too much." She later told him off for ringing her at her work because she embarrassed herself by yelling in front of her colleagues.

A week later she made an appointment with another lawyer, Malcolm Mithral, and she took him to see this lawyer to get him to make another Will that gave me less, her children more and made her and Wayne joint executors. The Will was not signed at that time and Allen told me that while she was at the house picking him up to take him to the lawyer's office, Beryl took the copies of his two previous Wills that he had already made. He stated, "She found them in our bedroom, scooped them up and put them into her handbag, and that is the last that I saw of them." I often heard him asking her to give the previous copies back to him but she refused. She later denied all knowledge of ever having them.

13. 1999 Allen's Disease takes over his Life

In the years leading up to 1999 Allen's health was still somewhat okay. He occasionally suffered falls but as this had been happening for some years I did not consider it to be a major problem. He spoke to me about us getting married, but he felt that he was too sick to do that at the time although when he felt better we would make the arrangements with the proviso that no-one should know because he didn't want to upset his family. He never became well enough for it to happen. He could self-care although he required help with taking his medication, as he often confused his dosage. He began to suffer from hallucinations and would not believe that the things that he was certain he could see did not really exist. He often visualized our cows walking down the driveway to the street or mice running around the room. I took him to see Doctor Dendrite where he explained that one of the pills that he was taking, Kemadrin, caused this and he was taken off that medication and given an alternative.

In the 1999 March/April school holidays I went for a holiday to Canada for twelve days. It was a trip that I had booked the previous year and we were both going. I renewed Allen's expired passport .and filled in the US visa application for him as we were going via Las Vegas. As the date for us to leave drew near, he became increasingly apprehensive about going. He ended up too distressed worrying about his health and being so far away from his doctors and home that we decided to cancel the trip. Then he insisted that I should still go as it was only for a short time. He would be quite fine at home but I had to be careful and look after myself, as he would not be there to protect me. He was still able to self-care and usually he was able to look after the farms, provided he took his medication properly. My son, who no longer lived with us, lived nearby and he was going to check on him regularly.

I had prepared Allen's daily medication dosage in labelled containers with the day, date, and time to take them on each one so that he could take the correct dosage at the correct time on the correct day. The containers were lined up in order on top of the plate cupboard in the kitchen. While I was away he mixed up his pill taking regimen and his health went into a rapid decline. He fell, so he tried ringing my son to get help from him but Luke was at work and did not answer the phone. Next, he tried ringing his daughter but she was also working, so he finally tried Wayne's number; he was self-employed and was always available. Wayne came to the farm and took him to their Brighton home, where he stayed until I returned (about ten days later).

While he was staying in Brighton he signed the latest Will. The witnesses were Beryl and Wayne. Beryl later claimed that while he was staying with them he asked to sign the 1999 Will that she had him make because he wanted to keep the Will secret from me. As I was away, he felt that I would not find out about it but, he had already told me about the Will change before I departed. After my return, he got me to write out a cheque and mail it to Beryl. He said it was to reimburse her because she paid the account to the lawyer who drew up the Will on his behalf. He had no intention of keeping the making or signing of a new Will secret from me because he felt that the 1999 Will was not right, as Beryl and Wayne were the witnesses to his signing it. He was also not happy because he did not want Wayne to be executor and in control of his money. He still harboured feelings of resentment toward him. Around this time, he told me that they were suggesting to him that he should be setting up a family trust to reduce the tax he was paying.

A simplified explanation of a trust suggests it is a type of company that belongs to a family. A person can put all property and assets into the trust and share ownership with some or all members of the family. No individual owns any of the property; it belongs to the trust but they can receive property rental income from the trust. When a person dies, because he or she has transferred all assets into the trust, there is nothing left to gift to other people in a Will. The trust continues, with the dead person no longer being a member of the trust and the remaining trust members continuing to receive benefit from the assets owned by the trust. Allen did not want to put all his assets into a trust, as he wanted to maintain control of his own assets. I would not have been a member of the trust so I would end up with nothing of his if he died after setting up a trust.

Beryl also found a number of properties for him to invest in with her. All the properties cost a little over one million dollars, about the same amount as the cash money that he had in his savings deposit. He told me that she insisted that she needed more income and wanted him to help her out financially. Later she claimed that she wanted him to buy a house for him to live in that was near her place. He did not want to move to the city to live and wanted to remain on his farm. I drove him to Brighton so that he could see some of the properties that she wanted him to buy as investments with her. He did not want to buy any more properties because of the work that would be required to maintain them, and he never bought any of the properties suggested by her at that time. He always referred to real estate as the agony of owning property. Beryl did purchase at least one of those properties on her own and also bought some shops and offices in the main street of Brighton.

I discovered that Beryl claimed I was exerting an unacceptable degree of emotional control over her father, when in fact he was with me because I was not a controlling person. He often commented that he could not understand why we never fought with each other and that he regularly had arguments with May throughout their marriage, and he always ended up fighting with his daughter whenever he saw her. Yet at times he could spend twenty-four hours a day, seven days a week with me and we never argued. I find confrontation too stressful, so I avoid it whenever possible. Beryl could not understand that it was not emotional control that affected his feelings towards me but our peaceful life. He knew me better than any other person in his life, including my thoughts and emotions; he could almost read my mind because he was so close to me.

His life with me was very calming and he did not want to upset the harmony, so he tended to favour me. When a man enters into a relationship with a woman, it is totally his own choice and when a couple love each other, they are going to consider each other's needs before anyone else's. Beryl could not accept that he put me before her and her children and that he considered me to be the most important person in his life. I was loved more than her or her children and she could not accept this. I did not exert any control over him. He was simply happy being with me. While I was away in Canada and he was at her Brighton home she took him to see his specialist, Doctor Dendrite. Doctor Dendrite always wrote a follow-up letter to Allen's general practitioner with details of his wellbeing at the time of the visit. In his letter of April 14th, the date that Beryl took Allen to see the specialist, Dr. Dendrite stated, Allen is in a very bad way these days...It is certain that he regularly becomes very confused and I feel that Allen's days of independent living are coming to an end.

When I returned from overseas I rang Allen from the airport. I intended to go home first and pick him up from his daughter's on the next day, but he insisted that I come to her house immediately to pick him up on my way home from the airport. When I arrived, he was sitting by the front door waiting for me. He could not get into the car quickly enough. His first words to me were, "Oh! Good! You are here! I've had enough of this, let's go!" On the drive, home the first thing that he told me was how Beryl and Wayne had pressured him to sign the latest Will even though he didn't want to do it.

Beryl always implied that when her father was with me his health suffered because I did not care for him well enough and I made his life very stressful. After I returned from my holiday, I took nine months' leave from work to care for him as he was in such a bad way health-wise. He spent twenty-four hours a day, seven days a week in my sole care. On the 29th April, after he had not seen Beryl for eight days and was totally within my care, he again went to Dr. Dendrite's surgery for a consultation. This time he went with me. Dr. Dendrite's letter to Allen's GP stated, He is a lot better than when I saw him ten days ago. Three months later he had his next consultation with Doctor Dendrite. He had now been in my sole care since my return from Canada. Doctor Dendrite's follow-up letter to the GP was worded as follows: I saw this man this morning and was amazed at just how well he is. He is bright and alert, standing straighter, walking well and the Parkinson's disease is obviously very well controlled.

Judging by his medical reports, it seemed quite clear that Allen was in no way being intimidated by me. He was obviously very happy when he was with me. It was his daughter who was overbearing and controlling and causing him to be unwell.

In a later visit Dr. Dendrite told me Beryl declared that she was angry with me for going away and leaving her stuck looking after her father when she had made other plans that had to be cancelled. That one doctor's visit was the only time she ever took him to any medical specialist. Whenever he asked her if she could help get him to an appointment, she would tell him that she was sorry she couldn't help him; she had her own life to live and her own family to look after. He needed to get someone else to do it.

While I was on leave from my work in 1999 I often took Allen out driving. We went on nostalgia trips to see many of the other farms and properties that he had owned in the past and we also visited his sister a few times. He had stories about each property that he told me as we drove by. He talked about the neighbours that he had when he lived on the places and lots of other trivia. One story that he recounted was about spraying the blackberry plants on his Smith's Gully farm. The house where he and May lived was at the top of a hill and the blackberry plants were growing in a gully at the bottom of the hill. They sprayed them one day and a couple of days later they saw a family walking around on their property picking and eating the blackberries off the plants. They tried yelling out to the people not to eat the berries but the people did not hear them. They were too far away and they left as soon as they saw Allen and May running down towards them, yelling, "Don't eat the blackberries!" May always hoped that they were alright and not poisoned. The sprays that they used were 2,4-D or 2,4-dichlorophenoxyacetic acid and 2,4,5-Trichlorophenoxyacetic acid (2,4,5-T). These products that are often referred to as 'Agent Orange' are linked to nervous system damage. Allen continued to use these products to spray the blackberry plants on his Cranbourne farms. He had some large drums of the stuff and he intended to completely use them up before he purchased any other chemical. He never covered his body or used any form of breathing protection when spraying. The directions on many farm chemical containers stipulate that users should shower and change their clothes after using chemicals, particularly before eating food. He never showered after he had finished spraying; he did not worry about having chemicals on his skin. He would sit down and eat his lunch after only giving his hands a cursory wash.

On one occasion when they were spraying May developed a severe breathing problem and she looked seriously unwell. I was driving a tractor, towing a trailer that held the spray chemicals in large drums. Allen was riding on the trailer supporting the spraying pump and hoses, and May was walking along with a hose spraying the weeds. She collapsed, wheezing and coughing and was on her hands and knees with the top of her head pointing towards the ground, coughing frantically. She was like this for about ten minutes. After she recovered, Allen and May swapped jobs and they continued to spray. They did not give much thought about whether using the chemicals caused the problem that she had experienced. Life just carried on as usual. They also had a sheep dip on the farm where they lived. A sheep dip is not fun for them; they are forced to take a swim in chemical-laden water to kill their body lice. The sheep were regularly dipped in an arsenic-based sheep dip chemical. There were also had a few containers of Asuntol arsenic-based dip stored in a cupboard inside the house. Neither Allen nor May ever used any preventative chemical exposure protection when handling the wet sheep or when they bailed the old chemical infused water out of the dip to refresh it with new water and chemical. The farm chemical use was never monitored. They did not purchase any new, more modern and maybe safer chemicals. They continued to use up whatever they had stored in the cupboard in his house. Chemicals that were left over from their earliest farming life in the 1950s included another baddie named Carbon Tetrachloride that was used for worming the sheep. If a high enough quantity of the vapour from this chemical is breathed in, it affects the central nervous system and can cause cancer.

Other chemicals that they used were Diazinon, which was put on the sheep to kill fly maggots, and they soaked the sheep's feet in formaldehyde. They had the chemical on their skin and breathed it in. I could not cope with the latter two chemicals. When the lid was taken off the Diazinon container, I immediately got a severe pain in my head from the aromatization of the ethers in the chemical. They didn't believe me and thought that I was imagining it. I decided that I would stay clear of the chemicals and let them do the chemical handling. Some years later I read a 'Materials Safety Data Sheet' on Diazinon; one of the symptoms of Diazinon poisoning in humans is severe headache. I wondered whether any of these chemicals contributed to Allen's illness. The chemicals in 2,4-D and 2,4,5-T are known to cause nerve damage.

Due to his failing health, in 1999 I carried out a lot more of the work involved with the running of the farms. He insisted that I do this, as he was losing his strength and could not do the work anymore. There were very few cows left, and the farms had long grass everywhere. I increased the number of cows that we had, as the original stock was becoming too old and some had died from old age. I went to the local auction sale yard and bought 120 cows. We each paid half of the purchase price and jointly owned the cows. Over the next few years we bought and sold more cows together. As I was going without wages while on leave, he thought that this was a good idea to compensate me for my loss of income.

Because he was finding it increasingly difficult to concentrate on managing his financial affairs, from 1999 onwards he made me do all his bookkeeping and manage his financial dealings. I was no bookkeeper and I found the task very time consuming and stressful, but he was adamant that I do it. He would tell me, "You have to do this for me because I can't do it. If you don't do it Wayne will take over and I don't want that." He would emphatically state, "I don't want Wayne to have anything to do with MY money!"

14. Allen Becomes Impossible to Manage

From the year 2000 Allen began developing a few other health issues in addition to his Parkinson's disease. He was becoming more demanding for care and needed a walking stick to help him maintain his balance. He could not rise to a standing position from chairs anymore, and was constantly getting me to pull him up. This was not easy, as he was very heavy. At the time, he weighed about eighty kilograms, which was too much for my fifty-four kilo weight to counterbalance. The pulling strain on my wrists was intense, causing me a lot of pain. I would have to hold his walking stick with two hands and get him to hold the handle so that I could pull him up because I was getting very purple, bruised fingers from his hands gripping too tightly onto mine. Regardless of the large amount of money in the bank and a very good income, he would not willingly spend any of it to make his life easier. I tried to get him to buy a chair that rose and tilted by electric motor to help him to a standing position, however he felt that such a chair would not help him and it was a waste of money. He insisted that it was not that difficult for me to lift him and I just needed to put a little more effort into helping him. Eventually I found a very cheap electrically operated chair for sale in a large department store, and I managed to get him into the shop to try out the chair. He decided that he liked the chair and he liked the price.

With that chair, he could get up as soon as he wanted and he realised that it would make his life easier. If he had the chair he would not need to call out and wait for me to come and help him all the time, so he bought it. The chair was a great purchase. Modern technology came to the rescue. If a person is going to be unwell, this era is the best time in all of history to be sick.

His sense of hearing, which had already been poor, was becoming much worse. Getting him to buy a hearing aid was a major project as hearing aids are not cheap. I would take him to a hearing specialist to have his hearing tested and his ear would be measured for an aid but he would not actually buy it as he was always in denial about his health problems. He complained to me that my diction was poor and I did not enunciate my words succinctly. If I worked at improving my speech and spoke a little louder he would be able to hear perfectly. I was already speaking as loudly as I could, and communicating with him often gave me a very sore throat. Every sound had to be at a very loud volume for him to hear. The volume on the TV was always turned up so high that I found the noise very uncomfortable and I had to wear small industrial hearing protective ear plugs whenever I was inside the house.

Conversations were carried out at a yell, usually with a few repeats until he could work out what was being said. The hearing aid was finally obtained, but it took a lot of visits to hearing specialists. After he got the aid he refused to pay for it for many months, until the company started to become quite threatening over his non-payment of the bill. He complained that he would have gotten a free hearing aid if he had only been enlisted as a soldier and fighting in the war all those years ago when he was a teenager, as war pensioners received them free. He really needed two aids, one for each ear, but he only bought one. Unfortunately, because of his Parkinson's disease he had an excess of ear wax production, which constantly blocked the workings of the aid. I had to regularly return it to the provider to have it cleaned. He was without it as often as he was with it. I felt that if he had two he could have alternated them between cleaning and using, but that was not to be.

Allen's night time waking was becoming more of an issue. He was extremely resentful because he was unwell and everyone else was healthy, and wished that everyone else could be sick like him. I kept telling him that it would not be of much benefit if I was to become sick also, as he would not have me to look after him, but he still was very resentful. He would wake up about every two hours during the night and start yelling out nonsense words. His favourite was to repeatedly call out very loudly "POCO LOCO." I never had any idea what his reasoning was behind this oral outburst, and he denied ever saying it if I asked him during the day. Once he was fully awake he would get up out of bed to go to the toilet and demand that I also get up. As he napped constantly during the day he could exist with this sleeping pattern, but I could not. Often, he could not wake me so he would stomp around the house yelling nonsense phrases and hitting the walls with his walking stick. BANG! "I need help." BANG! BANG! "You won't wake up!" BANG! BANG! BANG! "Where's that rotten daughter of mine? She doesn't do anything for me." BANG! BANG! "No one cares about me." BANG! BANG! "Ahh, haa ha haa, POCO LOCO." BANG! BANG! "Look out! Look out! I'm coming through! Ahh, haa ha haa." BANG! BANG! BANG! He tried hitting me with his walking stick which usually did wake me unless I was too sleep-deprived. I would only be able to remain awake for a few minutes, and I would fall straight to sleep again.

He stormed around the house for about fifteen to twenty minutes, until he had exhausted himself, then he would drop onto the bed and sleep for an hour or two. When he woke again, he would get out of bed and repeat the whole process. This would happen three or four times in a night. During the day time, he would not believe that he was creating such a ruckus during the night and that the bruises on my body were caused by him hitting me with his walking stick. One night I tape-recorded him but he still would not believe me. His night time activity would continue like that for three or four nights and then suddenly he would sleep through the whole night for the next few nights.

They were the most blissful nights. His nightly yelling sagas continued until May 2002, when he was on a nocturnal rampage and overbalanced while swinging his walking stick around. He fell, fracturing his shoulder, I was not entirely sure of the circumstances of the fall. I was woken by the sound of him crashing on the floor and a style of yelling that had changed. My subconscious mind registered that this time the noises were different and I woke up. He had to go to hospital in an ambulance and spent three months in a rehabilitation centre. While he was there he had physiotherapy to help him to walk and balance more effectively, and they made him use a wheeled walker.

When he returned home he was a lot more subdued and used the wheeled walker to get around the house. It was recommended that he buy a walker for himself but again he was in denial of his need. He refused to pay for the first walker that was sent home with him from the rehabilitation centre and they took it back. After a few weeks of trying to walk as before with his walking stick and falling a few times, he agreed that maybe he did need a walker. I found a walker style that he was happy with and bought it. It had very large, fat wheels that could travel over the rough ground outside the house. That walker was used for the next few years, until the last couple of months of his life.

Also at about this time his ability to follow a process became severely diminished. This became evident when he was unable to use the microwave oven. The controls were in a digital form and he had to press buttons to select the cooking program and to set the timer. He made me teach him how to use the microwave every day. I would have to painstakingly go through the steps repeatedly, but he could not do it. He would become very angry with me because I was not giving him good instructions and would say, "I could do it myself if you would only teach me how to do it but you don't want to show me!" This was so frustrating for us. I felt helpless. I was trying so hard to show him but he was unable to comprehend my instructions. I had owned the microwave for about fifteen years and he had been using it throughout the whole of that time, but suddenly he could no longer manage to operate it. Once again modern technology came to our rescue in the form of a very cheap microwave oven. It had two dials that were turned to operate it. One dial was to control the cooking power and the other dial was the cooking timer. It didn't even have an on or off button.

When the cooking timer was turned past zero time and the door was shut the microwave operated. When the door was opened the microwave stopped cooking. I left the dial turned for the longest possible cooking time and left the door slightly ajar. All he had to do was put his food inside and shut the door. When he thought the food had been cooked enough he opened the door and left it open until he wanted to use it again. He adjusted to using this microwave very quickly and soon forgot that we ever had any other microwave in the house.

15. Allen Needs More Help

Allen developed arthritis in both of his shoulders, which was a major problem because he could not easily dress or undress himself. We visited many doctors and tried several treatments to help him cope but none were very successful. His Parkinson's caused him to lose muscle tone, which meant that the usual treatment for his problem, a shoulder joint replacement, was not suitable because he did not have the muscles to hold the new joint in place. Due to his inability to use his shoulders he needed help to put on and take off all upper body clothing. In addition, he needed assistance to shower each day. The constant strain on my joints was taking a toll on my body. Mainly due to his size, I started developing problems with my elbow and shoulder joints.

I arranged an in-house carer to come in for forty-five minutes every morning to bathe and dress him. By the early 2000s, after I returned to my job, I found that he needed more care and I got him another carer to come in the late afternoon to help him put on his pyjamas. Eventually he needed a midday carer as well. These people coming into the house during the day were well able to form an opinion on our relationship and compatibility with each other. I got along very well with the women. They were often with Allen during visits from Beryl or Wayne while I was at work.

I never questioned the daily carers about these visits. Whenever I saw them, the carers often volunteered information to me about things that they overheard being said to Allen or comments/questions made by either Beryl or Wayne to them concerning me. Later, when he was in the nursing home, Wayne regularly questioned the nursing home staff about the standard of care I gave him when he went home to the farm with me for the day. Again, I never asked them anything; they would simply tell me and they made it clear to me that as far as they were concerned, they did not have any concerns about the way that I was looking after him. I was very upset over the things that were being said behind my back, but there was little that I could do about it. I got the general impression that both Beryl and Wayne were trying to give me a reputation that was entirely untrue.

In the years of the early 2000s Wayne would call in every few weeks and take Allen for a drive to visit one of his farms in Gippsland. I thought that it was good for him to get out for a few hours during the day, but he was constantly complaining about these trips. He repeatedly complained about Wayne and his way of conducting his own business affairs. He did not like the things that he was told during these drives. He recounted a telephone conversation that Wayne had while they were driving. One of Wayne's clients who was having taxation problems rang him to seek advice about what he should do. Wayne cut him off short, informing him that he was not working that week and would be in touch with him the following week when he was back in the office. After hanging up the phone he turned to Allen and sneeringly stated "Call someone who cares!" He told me some of the things that Wayne wanted to do with his own estate, and made it clear that he was not happy about what was being said to him. When I arrived home from work in the evenings he would grumble, and say things like, "Wayne is only out for himself. He only does things that will benefit him."

Because of the things that were said during these drives, Allen became very uneasy about his son-in-law being one of the executors in the will that was made in 1999. He did not want him in control of his estate. He decided that he wanted to change that Will but he did not like the idea of spending any more money on making a new one. When I had to pay his bills, I would write out the cheques and he would sign them, as this was his way of keeping control of his finances. I would then drive him to the local post office to pay the bills. He usually sat in the car while I went inside, where there would be a few free newspapers available for the taking. As he was always very keen to read the newspapers I would take them out to him to read while he was waiting for me. I never read the papers myself and relied on him to tell me about anything interesting that was written.

One of the papers had an advertisement that was placed by a local lawyer who was prepared to make Wills for a very nominal sum of $36.00. Allen, being very keen on bargains, rang the lawyer and made an appointment to make a new Will. He made me drive him to the office at the appointed time. I took Allen into the lawyer's office, and the lawyer, Carlita Vargos of Vargos and Partners, suggested that I go shopping or something and come back in an hour. She told me that she wanted to talk with Allen in private to be sure that he was making the Will of his own volition. When I returned they had finished their business and were talking about Allen's farms, and about my Siberian husky dogs. Carlita coincidentally also bred dogs, Rhodesian Ridgebacks, and showed us photos. I told her about my own dogs and the sled dog racing club that I competed with. She was a member of a different dog club that did an activity called tracking. This club had no connection to mine, which was why we had never met before.

In the Will that was made on that day Allen made me joint executor with his daughter. He told me that he wanted me to be an executor with Beryl so that I could carry out his wishes in the way he wanted. I really did not want to be an executor but he was insistent so I reluctantly agreed. I made the decision that I did not want anything to do with handling Beryl's side of the estate. If I was to be the executor I would ensure that my side was looked after and then hand it over to her to finalize the estate for herself and her family, although I didn't tell this to Allen.

Four further Wills were made with Carlita and her firm over the next few years. The next time that he changed his Will, it was after a discussion with his sister about their Wills and estates. She told him that he should be looking after me more in preference to his daughter. She felt that the children could look after themselves and the partner should come first, because that is the person who is giving up her lifestyle to look after him.

The Will change that happened next was due to Allen becoming displeased with both Beryl and Wayne. He felt under pressure from them to give them control over his estate and their apparent displeasure over the amount that he was gifting to me. He told me that

Beryl claimed he was being too generous and kept telling me, "If they are not happy with my Will they will tear it up. I am going to make you sole executor so that they cannot get the original." He also wanted to give me both farms. "Beryl does not need a farm," he would often say to me. "I want you to have both farms." I told him that I did not want two farms and if he gave me both farms I would sell one so he might as well leave the farms willed as they were. He decided that he would increase my share of the residual estate and make me sole executor.

The next Will change with his lawyer was made in early 2006, after he became a resident in a nursing home. Beryl took him again to change his Will to something more like she wanted. Unfortunately for her, Carlita would not let her stay with Allen while the Will was made, so she could not dictate the terms as she wanted them. The Will was signed although only slightly changed, taking one of the blocks of flats off me and sharing the entire residual estate excluding the farms four ways: one quarter each to Beryl, her two children and me. I was to still receive one farm and Beryl would be given the other one.

Allen often warned me about how his daughter and son-in-law would treat me after he was gone. "They will be ruthless toward you. Don't give into them. You never stand up to people, you always let people walk all over the top of you, but this time you will have to stand up to them. I only hope your lawyer will be tough enough to back you up."

16. Allen's Health Declines Even Further

By 2004 Allen's health and strength were declining rapidly. I took more leave from work. Doctor Dendrite was insisting that he should be placed into a nursing home as he needed a much higher level of nursing care than one person could provide. Allen did not think that he needed to go into a nursing home yet but it was evident that he was becoming almost totally dependent on other people for all his activities. His night time falls were happening more frequently. On many occasions, I had to call an ambulance in to get him up off the floor because I could not lift him. He often fell and ended up in awkward positions, which made the situation even more difficult for us both.

Once he fell sideways into the bath. His head was against the side wall, his bottom was sitting in the bottom of the bath and his legs were over the opposite side with his feet on the floor. Neither he nor I could do anything in this situation and help was urgently required. He was completely incapable of raising his own body when he fell if he ended up recumbent on the floor. During the daytime, I often had to call on our neighbours to come and assist me with getting him up. As he could not get himself up from a reclining position in bed we purchased an electrically operated hospital bed for him to sleep in at night. The head end of the bed could be raised into a sitting position. When I had him sitting up, I could swing his legs around over the edge of the bed to put his feet on the floor and there was an overhead hand grip to hold on to help him to stand. This was the only way that I could get him out of bed when he could not lift his own weight and I could not lift him.

His doctor was also insisting that a Power of Attorney needed to be appointed to act for him when he lost his mental faculties and he told me that Allen would not be making his own decisions for very much longer. Dr. Dendrite had told him that he needed to do this on many previous visits, but this time he was very adamant that this should be done urgently. He stood in front of him, looked him squarely in the face, and very sternly told him, "You need to do this NOW!" Allen reluctantly started the process of setting up a Restricted Power of

Attorney, and we started looking for a nursing home that could care for him.

It took many months to find a suitable nursing home. Most required the patients to pay a bond before they could move into the nursing home. The bond was calculated using a person's wealth. In Allen's case, the bond amount was four hundred and fifty thousand dollars. The bond was invested on behalf of the patient and the interest and some of the capital was used to cover the person's residency costs. In addition, the patient had to pay a monthly amount. Allen did not want to pay a bond. A person on a war pension did not have to pay any bond. The lack of war service was bugging him again. I had to fill in many application forms and photocopy four copies of each set of forms to submit to each nursing home. On the forms, I had to list contact details and the relationship status of Allen's relatives. I wrote myself in as the primary contact and partner with Beryl as his daughter and the second contact person. I was required to find a nursing home that was not too far from the farms and did not require a bond payment. Fortunately, I managed to find about four.

They were in older style buildings and seemed very basic to me. I preferred the newly built places with private rooms and facilities, but Allen would not pay the bond. I submitted applications to about six nursing homes: the four that did not require a bond payment and two that had a minimal bond of fifty thousand dollars. We then had to wait for a place to become available. All the homes had waiting lists and places did not come up until a patient died. In a nursing home this was likely to happen quite regularly. Patients rarely left in any other way, although sometimes a patient was transferred to another nursing home.

17. Allen Goes to Live in a Nursing Home

In June 2005, a telephone call came from a local nursing home and I took Allen to the home for a visit. We had a look around the buildings and found out about the activities and meals that were on offer. The staff seemed friendly and caring, while the patients appeared to be clean and contented. The place was conveniently located for me to take him out to the farms during the day so we filled in the paperwork and went home to pack. The first thing he did was ring his daughter. He did not sound too upset when he was talking on the phone but after he hung up he became very distressed.

He did not really believe that he should go into the home, and was becoming very angry. He started calling me names and telling me what a rotten person I was. It was a very distressing time for us. The grandmother of my daughter-in-law had recently died with Parkinson's disease. Her husband cared for her at home until she died. Allen could not understand why I couldn't care for him at home like her husband had done. He could not see the difference between a large 180cm tall man caring for a tiny 150cm tall woman and himself with me, where the carer to patient size/weight ratio was reversed. Had he been much smaller than me or even the same size, I could have been able to cope.

When I took him into the home we were both crying. I left him in the care of the staff and promised him that I would visit him every night after work. This promise I kept with him for the next eighteen months of his life. After I left the nursing home I felt alone and at a loss with what to do with myself. I went to the local shopping centre, where I tried to interest myself in looking at the clothes, but I could not concentrate. I realized that I would be alone at home. I had never really lived alone before in my life and it was a weird feeling. Allen went into the nursing home on a Wednesday and on Saturday morning, as I had promised, I arrived at the nursing home and took him home to the farm for the day. It was a mistake! He refused to go back in the afternoon.

The nursing home called and there was a lot of trouble because he had to spend his nights in the nursing home so that the nursing home management could receive government funding for his care.

They agreed that he could spend that night at the farm but he had to return by the following night. While he was at the farm he rang his daughter and talked to her for about thirty minutes, telling her all about the nursing home. On Sunday night, I convinced him that he had to return to the home, as I had to work the next day and he would be alone all day. I managed to get him to walk to the car and drove him back to the home, although he was very upset and seemed very depressed. I could not do or say anything to help him.

He felt trapped in the nursing home. The main door into the home was opened by a keypad which visitors keyed a four number code into to unlock the door. The code was clearly written in large digits above the keypad. By the time patients were admitted to the home they could still read the number code, but they were no longer able to key in the numbers to open the door. Whenever a new patient was admitted to the home he or she would stand at the door, looking at the keypad while trying to figure out how to open the door. They could understand that the keypad was important for opening the door, but they could not operate it. When we arrived back at the nursing home, he insisted that I show him how to key in the code to open the door. This was so that he could do it on his own if he needed to leave when I wasn't there. I happily showed him because I knew that he could never do it, no matter how many times he was shown. Often, when I arrived in the mornings to take him out, he would be standing at the keypad trying to key in the code so the door would open.

I continued to visit him every night and took him to our home on the three days that I wasn't working. It took some time for him to adjust to the routine, and often he would refuse to go back to the home. I would have to call my son to help me and with my son there to assist him, he would then walk out to the car like a lamb, not complaining about going back. In fact, he seemed quite OK about going. He only played naughty child with me although he eventually became settled into the nursing home and more resigned to spending his life there. He finally adjusted to going on the farm visits during the day times and spending nights in the nursing home. When I took him home he was willing to return in the evenings, knowing that he would be going out again very soon.

18. Another Will

In January 2006 Allen told me that Beryl found out that he had changed his Will since the 1999 version. I am not sure how she knew but I presumed that she may have telephoned the previous lawyer, Malcolm Mithral, and been told by him. Allen told me that she was very angry with him. He said that she became more insistent that he should set up a family trust so that they would not have to pay tax on his estate when they received it. She also was complaining that he was giving me the farm that she expected to be given when her mother died, and that at the minimum, she should have been given her mother's half share in that property. Allen and May owned the property as joint tenants, and May's share passed on to him after her death. Beryl claimed that her mother paid half the purchase price for the property, but she didn't.

Allen told me that whenever they had discussions about his Will, Beryl said things to him like, "Whatever you give Catherine you are really giving to some other man. When you die Catherine will remarry and some other man will get the benefit of the property and assets that you and my mother put together for my benefit." I had also heard her saying similar things. These conversations did have a major effect on his thinking, as he did not like the idea of me being involved with any other man; he was very jealous.

I kept telling him that I was getting very old and the men who would be interested in me would be even older. They would soon be requiring a nurse and I did not want to spend the rest of my life nursing an older man.

His visualisation of my future relationships and mine were totally different! On other occasions Beryl complained that my son, Luke, should not get the benefit of the property, as it was for her and her own children. This argument did not bother him as much, as he had spent a lot of his life with Luke (since he was five) and had a lot to do with his upbringing. His counter-argument was always that she should not expect an automatic right to his money. He should be able to do what he wanted with it and would state, "There is enough money for everyone."

While he was in the nursing home I was becoming quite unsettled by things that the staff told me. When I arrived in the mornings to take him to the farms a staff member would tell me about Wayne visiting and questioning staff about whether they felt he was being properly cared for when he went to the farm with me. The staff member would assure me that they had no concerns about my care of him when I took him to the farm for the day. I got the general impression that he was trying to instil a sense of unease in the staff about me. A notation in Allen's file mentioned that he was emotionally dependent on his partner. Staff had to ring me on his behalf so that he could talk to me and I could reassure him that everything was all right at home.

There were also unsettling things happening on the farm. I checked the cows every day to make sure that they were well, but on many occasions when I arrived at the nursing home after work Allen would tell me that Wayne had visited him that day and informed him that he had been out to the farms and there were sick cows lying on the ground, unable to get up.

There had been no sick cows the night before, and I would be puzzled by this. Sure enough, when I got home there would be a sick cow or two. It meant getting the vet out, and often the reason for the cow being unable to stand could not be worked out. Usually the cow would have to be destroyed because we could not find out what was wrong with it and it never recovered. Allen would be quite upset about all the sick cows that seemed to be on the farm, and I was baffled as to what was happening to them. When I told him that there were no sick cows the evening before, he began to doubt me. He kept saying that he never had so many animals getting sick in all his years of farming. It seemed unusual to me that the cows only seemed to become sick when Wayne had been on the farms. I was becoming extremely unsettled about the way things were looking.

There was talk that maybe I was incapable of running the farms on my own and they needed to be given to Wayne and Beryl, but Allen did not want the situation to change. He did not want to give control of his properties to his daughter and son-in-law. He always had the faint hope that he would get better and be able to return to run his farms himself. If he gave them over to his daughter, he would not be able to easily take them back when he was well again.

By early 2006 after he had been in the nursing home for six months, Allen's mental acuity had deteriorated. He had moments when he was completely off the planet and moments when he was just confused and moments when he was totally normal. His behaviour at times was like that of a naughty boy. He suffered bouts of constipation and diarrhoea and often soiled his clothes. He would go to the toilet by himself and if his pants were soiled he would take them off and walk around the nursing home without any pants on. The nursing home staff told me that he was often verbally disruptive and aggressive toward them and that he often threatened to hit staff. He was put on a managed care plan to try to modify his behaviour.

This was the time when the seventh Will was made. Ever since Beryl had found out that her father had changed his Will in 2004, she had become very insistent that he change it again. He informed me that she was adamant if his Will was not the way that she wanted it she would contest it, and also about her wanting him to change his Will when he was at the farm the weekend before he did it. He said, "Beryl wants me to change my Will but I am not going to change it. What I decided to do is how things will remain and I won't be letting Beryl tell me what to do." He also told me that Wayne had visited him and was renewing his efforts at trying to get him to set up a trust and put all his assets into it. He did not want to do it and said, "If I do that I will lose control of my things. They will have control and tell me what to do. Wayne will be able to do what he wants with my money. I don't want that." He insisted that he did not care about the tax issue that his family was claiming would be a problem if he didn't put his assets into a trust and he didn't really care about what happened after he was dead. He just wanted to be left in peace.

One Monday when I visited him in the evening after work he was in a confused state and seemed very distressed after a visit from Beryl. He told me that she had made an appointment with a lawyer in Dandenong for the next day but he was not going to change his Will. On Tuesday night when I visited he told me that Beryl and Wayne arrived at the nursing home with one of their sons but he was not sure which one. He was unable to walk so they got their arms under each of his shoulders and carried him to their car and drove him to a lawyer. They had to carry him into the lawyer's office. He said that he was not sure whether he had changed his Will or not; in fact, he was not sure what they had made him do. He was very vague about it all and said that he was not sure what he had done. Whether he made a new Will or started making a trust, he was not sure. Later, after he had died, I found out through court documents that they had been to Carlita Vargos' office and Beryl had refused to leave the room or allow her father to make his Will alone with his lawyer who had to insist three times that she leave. Carlita kept telling her that she wanted to make sure that her client was operating on his own free will.

I felt that I urgently needed to do something to protect myself. I had spent so many years of my life nursing him and had gone without holidays, wages and job advancement opportunities because of his care needs, so I believed that I was entitled to be compensated. When a woman is in a situation such as mine, people are very keen to tell stories of women they know who have been in similar situations.

These stories were of women who ended up with nothing to show for the many years of being a dutiful partner and nurse to an ailing man. I did not want to be left without anything, like what had happened to the mother of a work colleague of mine. That woman had helped her husband run a dairy farm and worked as a nurse at the same time, using her wages to support the husband's farm. When the husband got sick she looked after him and continued to run the dairy farm during the day time and work as a nurse at night. When he died he left all his assets to his son by a previous marriage. The wife was left nothing and is now a pensioner being supported by taxpayers. The son's inheritance made him a multi-millionaire but he did not give his stepmother any consideration for her plight and even evicted her from the matrimonial home. I also heard about another woman that a neighbour knew whose partner's relative had the partner's assets transferred into his name before the person died. After he died the Will meant nothing, as the properties had already been transferred into the other person's name and were no longer part of the estate. I did not want to take my partner's assets off him; I merely wanted to make sure that they stayed in his name for the rest of his life.

On the following weekend, Allen told me that he felt sure he had changed his Will but he did not know which lawyer he had seen. I was quite upset, not so much because he had changed his Will but because he deceived me the weekend before when he said that he would not make any changes to his Will. Why did he have say that if he did not mean it? I could not understand what he was doing. He wanted me to make another lawyer's appointment and he would change it back, but I could not see any point in having him do it as I felt that Beryl would make him change it again. One week later we were paying the bills and Allen told me that his daughter had paid the lawyer's bill for him and to make out a cheque to her for $550 for reimbursement. I wondered why she had paid the bill and I felt that there was some sort of underhanded activity being carried out. They did not want me to know exactly what the bill was for or the name of the lawyer. This was a repeat of what happened when the 1999 Will was made. A leopard does not change its spots!

A Restricted Power of Attorney was made by Carlita listing both Beryl and myself as joint signatories. The power gave her and myself permission to pay any bills in Allen's name should he become no longer able to do them himself. The power would only come into effect after he was medically certified as being no longer able to manage his own affairs. We both had to be co-signatories to the signing of any cheques or legal documents. I thought it would be a difficult thing to achieve and hardly worthwhile, considering I was already doing virtually all the financial work anyway. I looked after his bank accounts and had his ATM card to withdraw money for him and to pay his bills without him having to sign cheques. I merely took bills to the post office and keyed his pin number in to pay bills whenever he was not well enough to sign cheques. He still wanted to be in control of his own finances, so usually we would go over his bills together at the farm. I would have the cheques pre-written out to save time and save him the mental stress of checking everything. I gave him the bill to look at and the cheque to sign. In the latter months of his life he was not always entirely sure of what he was doing and simply signed the cheques, leaving me to organize the payments, record keeping and everything else for him.

Around the time of the making of the seventh Will in early 2006, Allen told me that Beryl was complaining to him about Wayne having to pay a lot of back taxes to the tax department. She claimed that he owed three million dollars and they did not have the money to pay it. She did not know how they would be able to pay and said that they could sell assets but that would mean that they would have to pay even more tax on the profit made from selling off their assets. Allen told me that he did not feel any obligation to assist Wayne with money. I checked the Australian Taxation Office website on the Internet to see whether I could find any information about Wayne's tax issue. Considering the amount of money that was being suggested as owing, I felt sure that there would some written information in the Law Rulings and Policy section of the web site. This section gave background information and tax decisions that had been made about individuals and companies in the past. The names and details of people who had tax rulings made for or against them were removed, as well as any other identifying information. The filtered version was written up on this section of the Taxation website. People could check for similar situations to their own taxation query to see whether they could apply a similar ruling to their own situation. I found information on Wayne's father's tax ruling from about twenty years previously. It was a case that went to court and his father had lost the case. Allen had previously told me the circumstances of the case so I knew about it. I was amazed to find the information there had not been thoroughly filtered to remove all identifying information. His name was still listed, which is how I found it in the first place. I did not find any mention of any recently made tax decisions that could have matched Wayne's alleged tax situation. I secretly felt that it was a made-up story to get Allen to give them his money. Later, when he asked his daughter how they went with the tax bill, he was told that Wayne worked out a payment plan with the tax office and everything was now okay.

19. The War Begins

I was in a dilemma. I believed that Wayne and Beryl did not want me to have the farm that I was promised. I needed to do something to protect myself for my future. I had no property of my own because Allen did not want me to have independence from him. I sold my own home at his insistence and never bought another house because he kept telling me that I didn't need a house. Whenever I found a house that I wanted to buy as an investment for my future he always found something wrong with it. I had invested well over one hundred thousand dollars of my own money into the farm that I lived on, repairing and maintaining it, because he insisted that I should take over looking after it and paying for its upkeep, as he was giving it to me in his Will.

I was having health problems as a result of looking after him and I did not know whether the problems would become worse, making it difficult for me to earn my own living. In 2002, I discussed my situation and concerns with a work colleague of mine who was teaching part time and while studying part time for a law degree. She offered to have a chat with one of her lecturers at Melbourne University to see if she could get me some advice. Her lecturer gave her the contact details for a firm of lawyers in Melbourne city, Macafferty and Co. This legal firm specialized in family law matters including de-facto relationships. I made an appointment and spoke with Oona Macafferty, a lawyer from that firm. Oona suggested that I have a talk with Allen about my concerns and she wrote a letter of proposal for him, suggesting that he should consider signing over to me the property that he intended to leave me in his Will. This letter seemed to be similar in content to the one written by Wayne that Allen found in May's bag after her death. I recalled how angry he was when he realised Wayne had obtained legal advice about May's property. I did not want to have any sort of confrontation and could not face having any arguments, so I did not go ahead with the letter or any other legal plans over his estate.

I obtained advice on what were my entitlements as his domestic partner and what steps I could take if I felt that my financial security was under threat from his family. I never told anyone about my meeting with the lawyer, however I quietly broached the subject with Allen, telling him that I wanted the farm where I lived to be transferred into joint names, as he had promised to give me that property anyway. He said that I was getting it in the Will and assured me of that, so it was not necessary. His words were, "I've made a Will; that should be enough." I was not convinced but I went along with it. It turned out I was right in thinking a Will would not be good enough to provide me with security.

After the new Will was made in February 2006, I thought about what he had said to me two days earlier, assuring me he had no intention of giving in to his daughter and changing his Will. I was upset and worried about myself and my future. I was the one who had given up fourteen years of my life to look after him during his illness, not Beryl or Wayne, and I felt that I had a right to be treated equally in his Will. He assured me that he did not think that he had changed his Will; he only altered it slightly and told me that he would change it back if that was what I wanted. I said to him, "You will make a new Will to suit me and then you will make another for your daughter to suit her and then change it for me again and it will end up being a case of which Will is in force when you die. It seems like a pointless idea to me so don't bother. I am going to do something to protect myself because although you have taken care of me very well until now, after you are gone I will be on my own. I have to take steps to protect myself."

I made an appointment with Macafferty and Co, the same law firm that I saw back in 2002, and got further legal advice. This time caveats were put on all of Allen's properties. De-facto proceedings were started and I felt overwhelmed by the speed with which things were happening. I wanted to move slower and gradually start the proceedings when Allen became totally unable to understand anything, but the lawyers were very convincing. In hindsight, it was a good thing for me that I had taken these steps at the time.

After Allen died I could not be evicted from the house or off the farm because of my de-facto proceedings. I told him about my visit to the lawyers and what I had done as I am not a very secretive person. He was quite angry and the next day when we were at the farm he got me to dial Beryl's number so he could speak with her. When she answered he said, "You've really opened a can of worms now!" and proceeded to tell her about what I was doing. It was a brief conversation and after he had hung up the phone we sat and had lunch. I was not interested in discussing the matter further. What was done was done and hating confrontation, I was happy to continue with our lives the same as before, visiting in the nursing home after work and taking him home to the farm on my days off.

I had no interest in discussing the case with him, and told him that there was no point talking about it whenever we saw each other. I said that it was something that could sit without progress until after he died and that I did not want any more than he had promised to give me, but I did not want to get any less, either. The caveats would stay in place for the rest of his life and I hoped that the proceedings could sit quietly in the background during his lifetime. Beryl and Wayne, on the other hand, took a very active interest in the proceedings and actively took up the case on his behalf. They sought legal advice and took legal representatives to meet and advise him. My lawyers were pushing on my side and I tried to sit quietly and wait as I wanted life to continue as before, but there was no chance of that.

20. The Lying Begins

One evening in August 2006, after arriving at the nursing home and walking towards Allen's room, I could hear Beryl talking to him about the de-facto case and how they intended to defend it. She was in his room with him and because of his hearing difficulty was speaking very loudly. In fact, she was yelling. I distinctly heard her telling him that they were going to claim that he never had a relationship with me to prevent my de-facto claims from proceeding. He was refusing, saying that it was fraud and he would go to jail and he did not want to go to jail. Her side of the conversation stopped the minute I entered the room. I said hello to them both but got no response from Beryl. She looked away, picked up her things and left immediately. I thought It seems that Beryl is somewhat shitty with me. Oh well, too bad!

On another occasion Allen told me that she had taken him to his lawyer, where the claim was made that he and I never had a relationship. He said that he refused and stated that he would not deny being in a relationship with me and was very angry with his daughter for trying to make him deny our relationship. He considered that it was an affront to his manhood for him to claim that he was not having sex and told them, "You expect me to deny that I made love to her three or four times a week." He boasted that they both looked rather shocked by what he said. He laughed at their reaction. He liked to boast about his bedroom skills so much that often at the end of a visit to Dr. Dendrite, he would turn to the doctor and say to him, "I can still 'Blow the Bishop', Doc." I always felt a little mortified at him saying this and I would ask him not to say it to people but he would laugh at me.

I found out later that Beryl had contacted her father's lawyer to try to get yet another Will made. She also wanted to remove my name from his Restricted Power of Attorney - because of the circumstances she felt that she could not share control over his assets with me. The earlier Power of Attorney was revoked and a new Restricted Power of Attorney was made at that time giving her sole control over the assets. This power would not come into effect until her father was certified by a doctor as being no longer able to make his own decisions. I was still looking after all his financial dealings until the certification happened as he did not wish to change the situation. It turned out the Restricted Power of Attorney never came into effect and I was in control of everything until the day that he died. I looked after all his properties, his financial bookwork and liaised with his various business professionals except for his lawyer for his de-facto proceedings. Although I had instigated the proceedings, he would not hand any of his financial dealings over to his daughter and son–in-law.

One evening in October when I was visiting, he told me that Beryl had visited earlier that day and informed him that Wayne had come up with a plan to stop me from getting anything from his estate. He pleaded with me to drop my case so that they would not use their plan. He said that he could not tell me what it was, just that I had to stop my proceedings or they would use the plan to ensure that I did not get anything from his estate. His words were, "You will get nothing! Please stop, they are very angry. If I sign over the farm to you, will you drop your case?" I answered, "Yes." The next evening when I visited, he told me he had informed Beryl that he intended to sign the farm over to me. He then declared, "Beryl wouldn't hear of it. She said that something could happen to you. You could die. If the farm was signed over to you and you die they would lose it." He went on to say that I wasn't safe living alone on the farm anymore and wanted me to get a new dog since all my Huskies had died of old age, as well as move someone else into the house to live with me. I racked my brains to try to find someone who could come to live with me. I thought of all the single women that I knew. With each one I had visions of two terrified women cowering under the bed. I could not imagine any one of them being a suitable body guard. I thought about the single men that I knew and decided that I did not want to move another person into my home. My life was already complicated enough.

He was making me feel very uneasy. He felt that as the man he was not looking after me as he should have been and was frustrated by his illness and being in the nursing home. He could not do anything to keep me safe. I was on my own. The Supreme Court ruled that mediation for the de-facto proceedings should be held to see if both parties could reach a settlement agreement. In early October, the mediation occurred. Beryl attended with her father, along with his lawyer and barrister. There was a mediator and I had my lawyer and barrister with me to look after my side of the meeting. It was the first time that I had attended anything like this and I felt that it was a very long, boring day. I knew that nothing would be achieved at the mediation but the court decreed that it should happen and so it did. Each party was in a separate room and the mediator moved between rooms to pass the information between us.

Beryl took control of Allen's side and it was clear that a mediator was not needed. She was yelling for most of the time and my lawyer, barrister and I could hear every word. Her father said nothing and later told me she did all the talking. I had a chuckle about this a couple of years later when I read a statement written in Wayne's affidavit that he wrote for the Will contesting case. He stated how he had suggested to Allen before the mediation that he should try the 'Holmes-a-Court' negotiating method. His method was to sit through and entire meeting and say nothing. Allen never ever mentioned this style of negotiating to me and I seriously doubt that he was even told such a thing before the mediation. He simply wasn't given a chance to say anything. Beryl did not want there to be any sort of settlement as she claimed that he was not in a relationship with me. There was the suggestion made that perhaps he was not speaking because he was not able to fully comprehend the proceedings. Also, there seemed to be a major differing of opinion as to the value of the assets. The farm that I was to be given seemed to be worth ten times as much as the other farm according to her. She seemed to change the values of everything according to whichever way the conversation was going.

At the end of a long and wasted day it was agreed that the mediation should be adjourned for six weeks so that the properties could be valued and for Allen to be assessed for his ability to understand the proceedings. A 'Heads of Agreement' document was written and signed by both parties stating that Beryl had to take her father to Dr. Dendrite to have his cognitive capacity assessed, because of his silence and the fact that many things had to be repeated to him. Often, he didn't seem to be able to understand what was going on therefore it was considered that he may have had difficulty following the proceedings.

She also had to obtain valuations of the properties. This had to be done before the next mediation. Both parties were to be given a copy of the assessment and valuations. A few weeks passed and nothing seemed to be getting done by her so I rang and made an appointment with Dr. Dendrite. I was to take Allen there three days later. I took him to the office and found that there was no doctor at the surgery. The receptionist told me that he was the only patient for that day and she had received a call the afternoon before telling her that he was too sick to attend and the appointment was cancelled.

I did not cancel the appointment so someone else must have done it on my behalf. I made another appointment for the next week and instructed the nurse to not cancel the appointment without ringing me to check. That appointment was kept but I never received a copy of the assessment report as was agreed to in the 'Heads of Agreement'. Allen's lawyer wrote to Dr. Dendrite instructing him to only send a copy of the report to her and I was not allowed to be told of the results. Despite the signed agreement stating that both parties should be given a copy, the capacity report was never given to me or my lawyer. I also obtained valuations for all the properties, as I was sure that Beryl would not do it.

Years later, when my lawyer subpoenaed Carlita Vargos' files I realised that my premonition was correct after I read an email from Beryl to her. The email stated that she did not want a statement of assets and liabilities to be made. The medical examination by Dr. Dendrite finally happened in November and the format of the assessment had changed from determining his cognitive capacity to give instructions in a mediation, to assessing his cognitive state for him to make another Will. I was not informed of this. Beryl had secretly arranged for this change. As I was not present during the examination I was not aware of what went on in the doctor's surgery. Dr. Dendrite's report stated that on the day of the examination Allen was considered to have sufficient cognitive capacity to make another Will if he was taken through the steps slowly and carefully.

The problem with the report for Beryl, was that Dr. Dendrite had asked her father about the members of his family. He told him me first, then his daughter and grandchildren. He asked him about his assets and how he wished to distribute them. He told Dr. Dendrite what he had and that he wanted me to receive half of his assets and the other half to go to his daughter. When I arrived back at the surgery to pick him up I chatted with Dr Dendrite and he said to me, "I wish you luck. You are going to need it!" That was the last time any of us ever saw Dr. Dendrite. Although he was still practicing and looked healthy at the time, the very unwell Allen outlived him!

21. Yet Another Will

Beryl's plot backfired because Allen clearly stated to Dr. Dendrite that he wanted to give half of his assets to me. At the same time, she wrote emails to Carlita saying that her father wanted a new Will drawn up with a completely different plan to the one stating his wishes that previously had been told to Dr. Dendrite. She wanted the new Will to give me one million dollars, payable at one hundred thousand a year over ten years, and I was to be written into the Will as 'a friend' only. A reply from Carlita to her suggested that this amount would most likely lead to me contesting his Will. So, she sent another email saying to give me two million dollars. This Will was drawn up as requested, although this amount was nowhere near half of his assets and totally different to what he had previously told Dr. Dendrite. Beryl was trying to write her own Will on behalf of her father.

Soon after this Will was written she met with Carlita and a barrister at the nursing home to discuss with Allen the contents of the new Will. He was very distressed when I arrived that afternoon. "They were here for over an hour today. We can't agree on who gets that farm. They are hounding me; I can't take any more. They are coming back tomorrow to make me sign it. I don't want to be here. You must take the day off from work tomorrow! You have to get me out of here!" The next day I stayed home from work because he had asked me to do so. I took him home to the farm and I did this at his request. According to the nursing home staff Beryl turned up at the nursing home during our absence. The staff told me that she appeared to be in a furious mood. I returned Allen to the home at about 4pm that afternoon with him being in a much calmer state of mind after spending the day with me. We never discussed the case or the Wills and all that day's conversations cantered on the animals and the farms. He really enjoyed being with me that day.

On the evening of the following day he told me that Beryl arrived at the nursing home after I had dropped him off the day before and took him to his lawyer's office, where he remained in her car while she went to get Carlita with the latest Will for him to sign which he refused to do. After the Will farce backfired she sent several emails to

Carlita with minimal offers to be made to me as settlement for the defacto case. Allen told me that he wanted to sign the farm over to me and he also wanted me to marry him. Beryl wrote different things to Carlita and suggested that her relationship with her father was still okay despite the ordeal that she was being subjected to. Other emails sent by her suggested that I was involved with a new man. The suggestion was quite ludicrous as to how I could possibly have a man on the side in addition to working, visiting Allen every evening, taking him home to the farms on the days that I didn't work, and looking after all his financial dealings, as well as managing six hundred acres of farms filled with livestock! In one of his follow-up letters to Dr. Dendrite, Allen's GP listed the work that I was doing and expressed amazement at how I was coping with all of that.

My neighbours knew that no other relationship existed. Farmers see what their neighbours get up to and whoever comes and goes onto the property. I was not involved with anyone. I had no intention of complicating my life anymore by starting a new relationship while Allen was still alive, and I certainly did not want to hurt his feelings in that way. Beryl was trying to upset him and trick his lawyer and her next suggestion was that they didn't think that I was even living in the house on the farm.

The next mediation, in November, was held in the city at Macafferty and Co.'s office. Prior to this mediation the parties had to submit affidavits stating their case. I outlined all the work that I had done over the years when I assisted Allen with the running of his farms, maintaining his flats and caring for him. Beryl's reply tried to turn it around by suggesting that none of it was work and that it was, in fact, all very easy and such fun-a bit of a lark, in fact. She herself even helped on occasions. In my memory, they were very rare occasions and once she complained that she had never been so tired in all her life after she spent a few hours on the farm helping her father.

The mediation was another wasted day as far as I was concerned. Allen did not attend, as he was not well enough. I went to the nursing home on my way into the city to pick him up. He was dressed and ready to go but he seemed a little weak. I thought of the difficulty that I would have getting him from the car into the lawyer's office, even though the home provided a wheelchair for him. I decided that nothing would be achieved at the mediation so I did not bother to take him telling him that it had nothing to do with him anyway. There was no argument between the two of us; the dispute was between Beryl, Wayne and me. There was no need for him to go. He seemed happy with this. I kissed him goodbye and he wished me luck as I left. Beryl and Wayne attended the mediation on his behalf. They were in a separate room from me but I could hear them yelling through the walls. Nothing was resolved on that five-thousand-dollar day, as I referred to the mediation days based on what they cost me.

22. More Wills Being Made

Allen's health was deteriorating. He was having bouts of chest infections, coupled with severe dementia attacks. He was still able to walk with assistance while using his walker. His hearing aid was failing and required servicing. Beryl visited him on a couple of occasions; I guess the only upside of my proceedings meant that she visited her father more often than she had ever done in the past. He told me that she had some legal documents that she wanted him to sign. One was a paper that she referred to as Wayne's agreement, a document which stated that there were four people to share the estate and that it should be divided equally four ways. He was very vague on the exact wording and he could not remember the exact contents of the document. I doubt that she gave him any opportunity to read it. She and her family were going away for the December-January school holiday period and she wanted him to also sign a document guaranteeing that he would not sign any property transfer or other legal documents in my favour while she was away. Allen said that he refused to sign anything for her. He was not entirely lucid during these times and he was not sure of the exact contents of the documents that she was trying to get him to sign.

At the same time Beryl was writing to Carlita, giving instructions to her to make a new Will, Wayne wrote his own letter with his version of the Will that his father-in-law wanted which was entirely different from Beryl's. Wayne's letter was submitted as evidence in 2011; in the letter, he suggested that Allen wanted a new Will made that divided the estate into four equal shares to be distributed to his daughter, me and his two grandsons. His daughter should be the executor and she was to be able to distribute the estate in whatever manner that she chose. Wayne wanted Carlita to make this Will and get it signed before Christmas. She did not get to see Allen before Christmas but did visit him in the nursing home in early January where she showed Wayne's letter to him. He told her that was not his wishes and refused to agree to anything.

It turned out that Allen, through his daughter and son-in-law, was in the process of writing three Wills at the one time: the one that was made with Beryl's help that he refused to sign; the one that Wayne wanted Carlita to make, which was the one that he didn't want, and the one that was allegedly made by Wayne's lawyer friend. This was supposedly signed at Beryl's home in February 2007, witnessed by their best friend, Ralph Daunton and his son, Steven. It is unlikely that Allen knew about these Wills. In addition, they had Carlita working on making a 'Court Made Will' for him on their behalf because she had informed them that she felt Allen no longer had capacity to make a new Will. So many Wills were being made at the same time, but none bore any similarity to his previously written Wills or carried out the wishes that he had told Dr. Dendrite at his assessment meeting in November. Whose Will was being executed here? Not Allen's! Wayne and Beryl tried to imply that I was trying to get the properties signed into my name, but this was not happening. I did nothing I didn't need to, as I had the properties tied up with caveats and they could not remove these.

It was in late November that Allen started talking about his funeral arrangements to me. He literally called out one evening when I was visiting, "Kew cemetery. I want to go to Kew cemetery." A few nights later he said, "The family grave. Put me in the family grave." I took this to be his instructions for his internment, so I went to Kew cemetery after work one evening and found the family crypt. It was too late to speak to anyone in charge of the cemetery so I rang the next day. I found that the family crypt had his grandmother and uncle already in there and there was one place available, so I started making the arrangements for him to be interned there as well.

December, it was the Christmas school holiday period. I was on holidays. I took Allen home to the farm on most days but not every day, as he was becoming too frail. He was no longer able to walk around the nursing home, so I took him shopping to buy a wheelchair. I had a problem with what to do with him at home, as I could not handle him very well on my own. The wheelchair made it possible for me to move him from the car to the house, but there was still the problem of transferring him from the car to the wheelchair when we arrived and back again when we had to return. He was too heavy for me to lift. His health was not very good and he was not entirely mentally lucid. His mental cognitive state meant he was not always aware whether he had been out of the nursing home or not. I persevered with taking him to the farm for as long as I could. As Beryl, Wayne and their children were away on holidays over Christmas and New Year they did not come and see him until early January.

23. Diary Notes Written during the Last Few Months of Allen's Life

Oona Macafferty advised me to keep a diary of daily events. The following is a chronology of events taken from the notations I made:

December 23rd, I bought a new water tank for the farm.

December 24th, I took Allen home to the farm and he sat in the car and watched me help the delivery man place the tank on the platform of the tank stand. After that I joined the new tank into the water pipes on the farm. He helped mentally and was quite proud of his achievement. He boasted to the staff back at the nursing home that evening about the work that he had done on that day.

December 25th, I took Allen to my son's place for Christmas dinner. He was able to communicate with everyone on that day but he could not use a fork or spoon so I had to feed him. He opened his Christmas presents but the whole outing exhausted him and he slept on the lounge for the rest of the day. I returned him to the nursing home in the evening.

December 31st, I did not take Allen out on New Year's Eve. I was with him at the nursing home as they held New Year activities there but Allen went to sleep early so I didn't stay until midnight.

January 1st, 2007, I did not take Allen out on New Year's Day. He was not well enough.

January 6th the cows were having calves and I took Allen to see the calves. January 9th, we had the grass cut to make hay and I took Allen to the farm on several occasions to see the hay rolls. He insisted that I sell some of them, as there were too many, and I was transporting them into the shed on my own using his very old Massey Ferguson tractor.

Allen repeatedly told me that I could have an accident and this was why he was not allowed to settle the de-facto proceedings, because Beryl said something could happen to me and they didn't want him to lose the property if he transferred it into my name and I died. I needed to be careful, he told me.

January 10th My neighbour Cameron met me at my front gate as I arrived home from visiting with Allen and told me that Wayne had been on the property during the day. I had arrived home early on that day because I was going to drive the tractor out to the hay paddock to move some rolls of hay into the shed. I regularly checked the tractor before I used it. I checked the oil and water levels and the tyres, as they kept going a little flat.

The radiator seemed to use water and regularly needed topping up; also, I would pump a little air into the deflating tractor tyres. While I was completing my check on the tractor, to my horror I discovered two of the eight wheel nuts missing from one of the back wheels of the tractor. The other five were completely loose and close to falling off. It gave me a big shock, as they were fine the day before when I used the tractor. I had to drive to the tractor repairers to buy new wheel nuts for the tractor to replace the two that were missing. The mechanic in the tractor shop told me that the threads on the screws or studs that the wheel nuts screwed onto would be shredded off if the wheel nuts had vibrated loose. I would need to have the studs replaced. He came out and inspected the tractor and said that the wheel studs were in perfect condition. They did not need to be replaced, as the nuts had not worked loose on their own. I bought new tyres, as they were the original tyres from when the tractor was new and they were in very poor condition. I was feeling very freaked out about using the tractor, particularly after the things that Allen had said to me about the possibility of me having an accident.

I did not tell him about the wheel nuts, as it would worry him too much. The original tyres had large cracks and holes in them and I was worried that they would develop a problem without me being able to detect anything, which is why I replaced them. It is most odd that eight wheel nuts could come loose on a forty-year-old tractor, as they were rusted in place. There are many farmers with tractors of the same vintage around the district and no one has ever had even one-wheel nut come loose or fall off, let alone eight. It was fortunate for me that I did my regular maintenance check on the tractor, resulting in me noticing the missing wheel nuts. If I hadn't I could have had a serious or fatal tractor accident. If the wheel had fallen off the tractor while I was driving it, it could have rolled over and crushed me. Beryl's prediction about me dying would have come true. The wheel nut incident and the things that Allen was saying to me made me feel extremely nervous. I sold the hay that was still in the paddock, as we already had more than enough hay stored in the hay shed and I became very cautious using the tractor from then onwards.

After the tractor incident, I bought an electronic automatic opening and closing security gate. I installed a keypad at the gate so that visitors could open it by entering a pre-set code. Unfortunately, I made the mistake of having an exit button that did not need a code to operate it on a post fifty metres up the driveway towards the house. Wayne and Beryl figured out that they only had to walk up and press the exit button to open the gate. This is what they did whenever they wanted to enter the property. I could not remove the exit button because Allen would not be able to go to the farm if he managed to get someone to drive him there during the day. He knew the code for the gate but he could not key it in, nor could he explain to someone else how to do it. I also installed two surveillance cameras around the house but I did not manage to capture anyone on the place during the daytime, even though Cameron regularly saw Wayne on the property. He obviously managed to stay out of camera range.

January 12th This was the last day that I ever took Allen out of the nursing home and home to the farm. He was becoming increasingly frail and I could not lift him when he needed to stand to get in or out of the car or to help him to go to the toilet. While at the farm I wrote cheques for Allen to sign to pay some bills.

From 13th January 2007, onwards Allen's frailty was so pronounced; the staff required a mechanical hoist to lift him out of bed and in and out of chairs. His mental cognitive ability was becoming very poor. He often confused where he was and what he was doing. He lost the ability to swallow readily and staff had to observe that he swallowed his medication when it was given to him.

January 17th, I wrote cheques to pay bills and Allen signed them.

January 23rd, I wrote cheques to pay the rates for the farms and blocks of flats and also paid the Nursing Home bill. Allen signed the cheques.

January 25th Cheques were written for the dentist, ambulance, Herald and Weekly Times, TRU. Allen signed every cheque but not all at one time, as he could not sign more than a couple of cheques at a time.

February 3rd in the nursing home, staff told me that Allen could no longer make a decision to change his body position himself; they had to move him during the night and get him to move himself during the daytime. He could only bear his own weight for short periods. They needed to use a standing machine for all transfers between his bed, the bathroom and his chair.

February 10th Beryl visited Allen. His hearing aid was not working properly so I put it into the shop for repair.

February 12th, I wrote cheques for the chemist and the other flats' rates and Allen signed the cheques. In the Nursing Home notes, it was noted that Allen was no longer able to walk and he had lost 5.05 kg in weight. He was no longer able to participate in social functions. He attended social functions as a passive observer only.

February 13th Beryl rang me asking about Allen's hearing aid.

February 14th, I picked up Allen's hearing aid from the repair shop.

February 15th, it would be Allen's birthday in two days' time, and Allen received a birthday card from his sister, which I read to him.

Allen's lawyer visited him in the nursing home to discuss an upcoming directions hearing. Allen did not recognize Carlita and was confused about what she wanted. He thought that his daughter was suing him for $80,000. She could not have any sort of meaningful discussion with him and left and later sent a letter to my lawyers saying that Allen should have a litigation guardian appointed, as he could not understand her. His accountant was suggested but Beryl did not want that. She wanted it to be her husband and she also wanted a new Will made. Carlita suggested that the only option now was a 'Court Made Will' and Beryl asked her to start the process. In hindsight, the deceptive games that she and Wayne were playing are now obvious. While things were going along with Carlita as if she was the only person involved in Allen's case, they were dealing with another lawyer in the background, Neville McNaughton. The right hand certainly didn't know what the left hand was doing!

February 16th, I wrote a cheque out to pay the Land Tax bill.

February 17th, it was Allen's 78th birthday. I visited him in the nursing home before I went to work. He was asleep so I didn't wake him. I visited him again in the afternoon after work to wish him a happy birthday and feed him his tea.

24. That Final Will

On Saturday February 18th, 2007 Beryl took her father to her home in Brighton for the day. He was slightly lucid mentally, although he was unable to walk and had to be physically lifted into the car by her and members of the nursing home staff. He had his recently repaired hearing aid, and it was working. I saw him at about 4.30pm, after she returned him to the home. He was in an agitated state and he said that they celebrated his birthday with a cake and everyone sang Happy Birthday to him. He had a pleasant day with the family until it was time to leave, when Beryl produced Wayne's agreement (possibly it was the last Will) for him to sign.

He said that he refused to sign anything without me being present and he would not sign it. He never mentioned that the agreement was a Will. I think that they misled him into believing that they were not trying to get him to sign a Will but an agreement stating that as there were four people to share the estate that each should get an equal share. That is how he explained it to me. He could never fully understand the contents of the agreement. He told me that his hearing aid was missing so I looked for it but I could not find it. I asked the nursing staff if they knew about it but they didn't and they noted that it was missing in their book.

After Allen died and the legal proceedings had finally progressed I read their affidavits where they claimed that he read the final Will and approved it on this day but did not sign it. They wrote that he told them that he would not sign it on that day as he wanted to leave it until later so that he could have a think about it. They claimed that they told him it was okay, there was plenty of time! According to Neville McNaughton's affidavit, he was told that Allen had approved the Will. Based on what had been said to me he did not approve any new Will on that day. Neville McNaughton decided that he was not happy with the way that the Will was written so he made what he claimed to be minimal changes.

There were more than thirty changes between the two Wills. The most significant one was where I was written in as a 'he' in the first

Will and a 'she' in the second. The fourth person named in the Will, who I presumed to be me, had the wrong last name. The second Will was much longer than the first. Nowhere in any of the affidavits was it written that these changes were authorised; it seems that Neville McNaughton did it on his own undertaking. The changes altered the tone of the Will and were quite significant. Allen's mental and cognitive skills were very poor during the week prior to the 26th, the day that he allegedly signed the final Will. Although it appeared that he was conversing quite normally and sounded clear and lucid, the conversations that I had with him were absolute fantasies.

February 19th Sunday morning I arrived at the nursing home at about 10.30 am and one of the nursing home staff gave me Allen's hearing aid. The plastic casing was crushed, rendering it unusable. She told me that it had been found on the floor under his bed.

I visualized a furious and vindictive Beryl deliberately stomping on it because he did not give in to her.

February 20th, I had arranged for an audiologist to visit him in the nursing home to test his hearing and make a mould of his ear canal so that his hearing aid could be repaired. He had his hearing tested on this day. The aid was not repaired at the time of Allen's alleged signing of the Will on the following weekend, so he would have had no chance of hearing details of what was being said to him. In the evening when I visited him he told me about his day. He had been fixing the fences on the farm and shearing sheep. I engaged him in a conversation, getting details about his work, and he tried to answer but then realised that he didn't know the answers. He agreed that he may have been imagining some of his day, but he assured me that it seemed very real to him. He failed to mention that he had a visit from the audiologist that morning and that he had a hearing test. I asked him about it but he had no recollection of it happening. He had completely forgotten about that. I had to check at the nurses' desk to find out if the test had been done.

Unknown to me at the time Beryl sent an email to Carlita where she claimed that while Allen was at her home over the weekend he had been perfectly mentally alert. I found out about this email some years later, after my lawyer had subpoenaed Carlita's files for the Will court case. When the files were submitted to the court I had access to them and I was able to read her email that was sent on this day. It appeared to me that she was setting up the scenario for the new Will to be signed. Perhaps she intended to use her email to Carlita as court evidence, should it be needed to prove that her father was mentally competent to make a new Will.

February 21st On Tuesday Allen told me that he didn't want to keep the wood splitter that he had bought, as it was too expensive. There was a lot more to the conversation, something about me returning it and exchanging it for something else and the like. I didn't recall all that was said to write down in my diary but the entire conversation sounded quite normal, even though a lot of it didn't make any sense. We had never owned a wood splitter but he did have one in the 1950s when he chopped firewood on his farm that he owned at that time. He was living on memories.

February 22nd the nursing home staff told me that he was no longer able to chew and swallow his food. He was put onto a diet of soft vitamised foods for all his meals. He was also no longer able to use a bottle for urinating so he wore adult incontinence underwear. He also had to wear a high absorbency incontinence pad overnight. He had to be repositioned every four hours during the night and he had to have someone encourage him to change his position every three hours during the day. He had reverted to being a baby again, with baby food going in one end and nappies for what came out of the other end.

February 24th On Friday evening when I arrived in his room he told me that the doctor had been to see him and that he had cancer. I was convinced that this had actually happened, as he had several skin cancers cut off in the past and he sounded quite convincing. I went to check with the nursing staff about this and they said that he was hallucinating constantly and they checked the records. I was told that he had not seen the doctor on that day or any previous days. One of the nurses said sometimes they were not sure which planet that he was on. The nursing home staff said that he often confused past and present events.

25th Saturday When I arrived, Allen was in an anxious state he thought that he had been at a cow sale and bought some cattle. As soon as he saw me he said, "Oh! Good! You're here! Quick! Help me to get up. I have just bought some cattle and they are locked up in the cattle yards. I need to get up and go out to let them go out into the paddock. It is too hot and they do not have any water. I need to let them out so that they can have a drink!" He wanted me to help him to stand so that he could go out and let the hypothetical cattle out of the cattle yards. I told him, "Oh! It's OK. I saw them there and I let them out." "Did you push them over to the water trough? They might not find it on their own," he replied. "Yes, I did," I said. "Did you see them drinking any water?" he asked. "Yes, they were very thirsty. They drank quite a lot." I replied. "What about the calves? Did they have a drink as well?" he asked. I thought the conversation was becoming very complicated. "Yes. The calves were with the cows and they had a drink of water with their mothers." He was concerned that they would not find the water trough on their own. After I had reassured him that everything was OK he calmed down and said, "I don't need to worry then. You have everything under control."

All this conversation sounded completely normal and would have been a conversation that he and I might have had five or ten years in the past. But none of it was real. He had not been to the cattle sale yards and bought cattle on that day; he was in the nursing home and unable to walk. He had no idea that what he was talking about was not true.

On that day, I read to him and fed him his lunch and dinner. He did not have a hearing aid and it was very difficult to communicate with him. To the best of my knowledge he did not see Beryl or her witnesses to the Will signing on this day. They did not come when I was there and the nursing staff did not tell me that he had had visitors during the day when I was not there. It is extremely unlikely that the Will dated 25 February 2007 was signed on this day. It certainly was not signed by him at his daughter's house in Brighton on the 25th February 2007. That was the date that was written on the Will in many places. Some years later in Beryl's, Wayne's, Ralph Daunton's and Steven Daunton's (the witnesses to the alleged Will signing) affidavits for the court case they stated that they made a mistake with the date. Nobody checked their mobile phone for the correct date, even though they stated in their affidavits that they had been contacted by Wayne on their mobile phones when he requested that they witness the Will signing.

On the following dates, 24/1/07; 31/1/07; 21/2/07; 28/2/07; 10/3/07; 17/3/07, he was being given antibiotics for chest infections. The nursing home notes for February 21, 22, 23, 24 and 25 stated that Allen was unwell and resting in bed for the whole of the day on these dates. Usually when he was unwell the staff would use a hoist and lift him out of bed to sit him in his chair. On these days, he was too unwell to sit in his chair. He was put on a Sustagen supplement and had extra fat added to his diet and put on 3kg by 7/03/07. He was also hand fed by me and the nursing home staff.

This is a summary of events in the week prior to the alleged Will signing. The interesting thing about his conversations was that when he was living in the past he could produce short sentences that were reasonably comprehensible. People who knew him could usually follow the gist of what he was saying, but when he had to have a conversation in the present he had difficulty verbalising more than a couple of words at a time. Conversations involving past events were already in his memory and could be spoken without him thinking about what he was going to say next. Conversations about present events required thinking on his part to find words to use and string together, which his brain seemed to fail him with doing. I was familiar with this type of conversation from my experience teaching people to speak English. English language learners could clearly parrot off pre-learned phrases without necessarily understanding what they were saying but carrying out a simple conversation on a topic where they did not have pre-learned phrases to use was very difficult for them. I am excellent at filling in conversational gaps, which meant that his conversations were not as clearly spoken as I have written them. If I had written them as spoken they would not have made any sense.

On February 26th Beryl took Allen to Brighton for the day. He did not have his hearing aid because it was broken and still being repaired. I drove into the car park at the nursing home at about 11.30am as I was going to feed him his lunch. I was not aware that he was being taken out for the day. Beryl had taken him out the previous Saturday, February 18th, the day after his birthday, and as she rarely took him out of the nursing home, I thought that she would not bother again for some time. When I arrived, she was there and she said that she was taking him home for the day. I did not go in and see him. I went home and returned to the nursing home at about 5.00pm to feed him his tea at 5.30. I arrived just after she had dropped him off and he was with Cherry, the activities coordinator at the home. He was feeling very distressed. Cherry told me that he regretted not marrying me and she suggested that I take him out in his wheelchair for a walk.

He was not exactly coherent about his day. He told me that he had a nice lunch and he saw his late wife May's sister, Myrtle. He watched his grandsons playing football. He never mentioned meeting Ralph or Steven Daunton, the Will signing witnesses, or having signed a new Will. For much of the walk he talked about cows and things but nothing that was entirely logical. After he and I had our walk we returned to the nursing home and I fed him his tea. He went to sleep quite quickly, exhausted from his day's activities.

25. The End is Nigh for Allen

For the last few weeks of his life, Allen was very unwell. He was having recurring chest and urinary tract infections and was on antibiotic medication for most of the time to try to reduce the severity of the infection. When a healthy person sits or lies down to sleep he/she will change their body position regularly to prevent pressure problems with the body's weight being in one place all the time. He could no longer reposition himself and the nursing home staff had to go to him every hour or so and move his body to a new position. This was done to prevent further health issues for him, such as bed sores. He could not grasp an object such as a cup, fork or spoon to have a drink or feed himself and had to be fed by another person.

His food had to be vitamised, as he was unable to swallow very well. As he could not swallow his medication his pills had to be crushed and mixed in liquid. He could not support his own weight, even to sit up in a chair and had to be lifted using a mechanical hoist. By this time, he could barely speak. It was while he was in this state of health that he allegedly signed his final will on a visit to his daughter's house in Brighton. The people who were present claimed that he conversed normally with them; sat upright in a chair; then independently picked up a pen and signed each page of the Will unassisted. He was surrounded by six people watching him sign: Beryl, Wayne, their two children and the two Will witnesses. One person stood beside him and turned the pages of the Will and held them flat for him. On reading about this I had a vision of six vultures standing over a corpse, waiting to devour it. In this situation, it was claimed that he was not stressed or under pressure; the whole Will signing was done in a relaxed friendly manner. This person doing the signing certainly did not sound like the Allen that was described in the nursing home reports.

February 27th One of the nursing home staff told me that Allen was very sick and he was unable to communicate lucidly. He talked a lot but his speech was unintelligible. Despite this Carlita received an email on Tuesday Feb 28th from Beryl saying how mentally alert her father was on his weekend visit to her home. I found out about this email years later when I read through Carlita's files. The nursing home staff said that Allen was in a very bad way but Beryl was trying to give Carlita the impression that he was completely well and mentally lucid on the weekend of the alleged final Will signing: 'very on the ball' was the wording used to describe his mental acuity. Carlita was in no way aware that the new Will had been made with Neville McNaughton.

March 3rd, I wrote cheques to pay the quarterly rates instalment for the flats, the chemist, Victorian roads vehicle registration, and the nursing home. Allen signed these cheques. After he had signed the cheques he mumbled, "The signature is not right! Check the signature." I replied, "The signature is fine." He said, "The signature is not right. Check the signature. I don't know what I am saying. Not that one. The other one! The other one!" I was confused by his words.

26. Allen Dies

On March 11th at about 10am I was at work when I received a call from the nursing home. I was told that Allen was dying and I should come right away. The staff asked me how they could contact Beryl, as her home telephone number was not being answered. I looked up her work number on the Internet for them. I then left work and went straight to the nursing home. When I got there, I was told that he was looking a little better than he seemed at the time that they had called me. He was sleeping, and I sat with him for about half an hour. I left the nursing home to go to the audiologists to pick up his hearing aid that had been repaired. I don't know why I saw it as important that I picked it up, I think it gave me a sense of normality, that everything was going to be okay and he was going to need it when he got better. When I arrived back at the home Beryl was there. She said that she had arranged for him to be transferred to hospital to have intravenous antibiotic treatment. She was waiting for an ambulance to come. I talked to his sleeping form and then told her I would go home for the time being and visit him in hospital later in the day.

Shortly after I arrived home Beryl turned up and told me that Allen had died in the ambulance and she wanted to have some clothes for his funeral, I went into shock, and without saying anything or showing much emotion, I took her inside and got one of his suits from the wardrobe and gave it to her. I tried to tell her that he wanted to be buried in Kew cemetery in the family crypt. I had already started to make the arrangements with the cemetery at his request. She adamantly stated that he was to be cremated and that was that. She claimed that he only wanted to be buried there because he thought his mother was there, but she wasn't. His grandmother and uncle were in the crypt and I felt that he should still go there but she did not agree. I decided to stay out of the funeral arrangements from that point on, it was already hurting enough. I had just lost my best friend who had entrusted me to his wishes and immediately they were being ignored. Beryl asked me to send all bills for the estate to her. She wanted her father's cheque book so she could pay for the funeral. I gave her a cheque book.

That afternoon I returned to the nursing home with my son and his wife to pick up Allen's personal effects. Beryl was already there, placing his things into bags. She told us that she was going to put his things into a charity donation bin. This was the first time my daughter-in-law had met her, although she had been married to my son for ten years and had known Allen for about twenty years in total. I'm sure the meeting and first impression was memorable.

After Allen's death, I was feeling totally alone and desolate. I did not seem to know what to do with myself. The daily visits to the nursing home that I had been making for the past eighteen months were over and I seemed to have a lot of free time on my hands. I went to the necropolis and paid him one final visit before the funeral. It was amazing to see him in death. The typical Parkinson mask that showed on his face in life no longer existed. He always had beautiful skin and his skin looked smooth and youthful, like it did when he was a younger man. It seemed very strange looking at him; he did not look like he was dead, just peacefully asleep. I touched his hand and it was cold. I thought about him telling me of the time when his grandmother had died. He was a small boy; his mother told him to kiss his grandmother's cheek and he said that she felt cold. I head an eerie feeling; as if his ghost was beside me. I asked the funeral director about the service the next day. He told me that everything had already been finalized.

My family came with me to the funeral. I was apprehensive about what would be said during the eulogy and upset because of the things that had already been said about me to Allen and various other people in the past. Some of my work colleagues attended, so I got my family to sit with my work colleagues. I needn't have worried about anything as I only got a two-word mention. I was not forward enough to say anything for myself, although many people said that I should have done so.

Allen's old school had kept in contact with him over the latter years of his life. About once a year someone from the school would come out to the farm to visit us. A representative from the school visited three months before he died. He wanted him to be a guest at a commemorative reunion for the big rowing championship team that he was a part of back in 1943. He would have liked to attend. I thought seriously about taking him to the event but it was to be held up on the Murray River, which was about three hours' drive away, and I felt that it would be too exhausting for him in his final state of health. I had to decline on his behalf. After he had died our neighbour, who had also had attended the same school, telephoned the school and informed them of his death. I received a very nice sympathy letter and an offer to publish a short valedictory piece in the magazine if I wished to submit something. My neighbour told me he would write something, so I found a very nice photo that could be included with the neighbour's submission. I sent it off to the school for inclusion with the written piece. The neighbour wrote about Allen's early life and about them being neighbours for over forty years. He finished with details of Allen's wife and his relationship with me after her death. Later, when the edition of the magazine was distributed, any mention of me had been omitted. It was as if I had never existed in his life.

A few days later I rang my lawyer, Oona Macafferty, informing her of his death. I had a meeting with her and we obtained a copy of the February 2006 Will from Carlita. A letter was written and sent to Wayne and Beryl informing them that I would cancel the domestic partner proceedings and settle on the February 2006 Will, provided that none of their family sought to reduce my share of that Will. A couple of weeks later Carlita sent a reply to Oona saying she had been sent a copy of what was claimed to be Allen's final Will signed and dated February 25th, 2007. This Will copy had been sent to her from the until then, unknown lawyer, Neville McNaughton. It seems that she was sacked from the case and Neville McNaughton was now handling legal matters for them.

This latest Will from Neville McNaughton decreed that Allen's estate should be divided into four parts and given equally to me, his daughter and her two children. His daughter was the executor and it was at her sole discretion as to how she was to distribute his assets. There was no set amount or specific property allocated to any one person. There also was a clause that stated that I would only receive my share of the estate if I had ceased all legal proceedings against him by the time of his death. If I hadn't, my share of his assets was to be given to his daughter and I was to receive nothing. As the proceedings had not been resolved, I was to receive nothing as per the clause. I was effectively cut out of the Will entirely.

There were two things about that Will that were not right. The first was the date. Two close friends of Wayne and Beryl's witnessed the Will. On the date that this Will was supposed to have been signed, Allen had been sleeping in the nursing home and I had been with him for most of the day. I went to the nursing home to check their records and I found that there was no record of the anyone else visiting him in the nursing home on that date. The next and most salient thing about the alleged final Will was Allen's signature. It was totally different from any other signature that he had ever produced before. The four signatures on the four pages of the Will were very identical to each other but they did not show even the slightest resemblance to any signature on any of his other Wills or to any other signature that he had produced on other documents. I was certain that this was not his signature!

From 1999 onwards I wrote out cheques for Allen's bills and he would sign them. In the last few months of his life I had to place a pen into his hand and place the pen on the line where the signature was to be written. His hand always moved from the initial place, and he was incapable of keeping it in a specific position. Over the last few weeks of his life, although he still signed his cheques, his signature had become very weak. He could not put any pressure on the paper and the ink was always very faint. His signature retained its recognizable characteristics but it was not neat, straight or written in a defined space.

He never developed the typical Parkinson's shake but he still suffered from something that Dr. Dendrite kept referring to as 'Cogwheel' rigidity, which causes a jerky movement as muscles tense and relax. To test this Dr. Dendrite would get him to twist his hands back and forth, wriggle his fingers, and move his hands upwards and downwards from his wrists. He would try to initiate the movements but at first nothing would happen then suddenly his hands would jump start into the movement. This was what happened whenever he tried to sign a document. His hand with the pen would be in position to start writing but it would jump to another position before he began writing.

The signatures on that final Will were dead-straight on the line, in a very defined, limited space, firmly written and very clear. His cogwheel rigidity prevented him from sequentially producing four such identical signatures and made it impossible for him to write on a line or to keep his writing within a defined space. The individual letters on the final Will signatures bore no resemblance to the letter formation in any of his other signatures.

27. Learning About Handwriting and Signatures

After I had seen the final Will I decided to research handwriting analysis. The Internet yielded a plethora of web sites with a considerable amount of relevant information. Being mindful that Internet information may not always be the most dependable, I also headed off to Monash and Melbourne University libraries and the State Library of Victoria. There are not many available books on the subject of handwriting identification however I located two that were very informative. Reading about handwriting proved to be very interesting, particularly the different identifiable characteristics associated with an individual's writing style. I was already aware that Parkinson's disease affects a person's handwriting as I had learned this in the creaky club meetings and observed it in Allen's writing.

The books had a section covering the effects of disease (including Parkinson's disease) and dementia on a person's writing style. The salient feature of a Parkinson's sufferer's handwriting was the term Micrographia. This was the tendency for the person's handwriting to become progressively smaller. The writer could start writing clearly and firmly, with the first two or three letters being well formed but after writing the first couple of letters the writing would progressively become smaller and less distinct. The pressure applied by the pen on the paper would decrease so that the writing would become less defined. This certainly described Allen's handwriting. Practice at writing does not improve this problem; it makes it worse. This also described his attempts at writing his signature.

Aware that his signature was deteriorating, he would try to practice on a scrap of paper before signing cheques, but two or three tries left him completely unable to write any consistent form of a legible signature. Whenever he signed cheques he could only do a couple at a time; any more would render his signature illegible. The book had examples of Parkinson's disease sufferer's signatures written before their diagnosis and signatures produced later, when their disease had progressed to one of the later more terminal stages. The progress of Parkinson's disease from diagnosis until death is defined in stages. The stages relate to the degree of functionality that is lost during the progress of the disease. Allen's signatures fitted the defined style changes perfectly.

Notwithstanding the Parkinson's disease changes, individual characteristics in a person's handwriting style are consistent throughout life. Two things affect a person's style of writing, the first being the learned patterns that are established when a person first learns to write. These patterns persist throughout life. Interestingly, the learned patterns are retained in people who lose the use of their hands and learn to write by holding a pen in their mouth or feet. The second thing that affects handwriting style is the size, shape and individual structure of a person's fingers, hands, arms and associated muscle composition. By studying the handwriting of close relatives many similar features can be found, mostly in letter shaping, size and spacing between letters. I was aware of this feature because over the years' people had commented on the similarity between my handwriting and that of my mother. I had never given it much thought until I read about it in the book.

The books that I read outlined the many features of letter formation; each feature had a name. The one that I found most relevant was the section on initial strokes. Initial strokes are considered to be a consistent feature of writing that does not change over a person's writing lifetime. In a Parkinson's person, the features of the initial strokes are retained. The first couple of letters written are the most consistent. There are many identifiable features for an initial stroke, it can be curved, straight, indistinct, etc. The one that I thought to be the most important in my situation was the starting position and base height of the left side of the initial stroke and the finishing position and height of the ending stroke on the right side of each letter. Some writers have the left side of the letter beginning lower and longer than the right and others write with the right side of the letter ending lower and longer than on the left side. Some writers have the base of both right and left sides of a letter sitting at about equal height but the lengths of each side could vary by alterations in the angular direction of the letter. For example, if the top of the letter was angled towards the right the base of the strokes could begin and end at the same height, but the left stroke could be longer than the right. I had hundreds of samples of Allen's signature, from the time he was a school student until just before his death. In his signatures, the initial stroke of the capital A in his name was longer and started lower on the left side than on the right side, unlike the four signatures on the final Will, where the right side was lower and longer than the left side.

He had always signed his name as A D Johnson and he never joined the first two initials of his name whenever he wrote his signature. They were always separate with diacritics (full stops) between them. In his signatures that were made in the final few months of his life the diacritics were difficult to distinguish and had to be viewed through a microscope or by making a 400 times photocopy enlargement, but they were still there. In the final Will of 2007 the letters A and D of the signature were joined together. If the signatures were examined using 400 times photocopy enlargement it was easy to see that the writer did not lift the pen between writing the letters. The two letters were formed as one continuous shaped line from start to finish, with no gaps and no diacritics. I looked through hundreds of examples of Allen's signature made during his lifetime and could not find any other example of his signature being written in this way. To my untrained eye the letter 's' on the Will signature also bore no resemblance to the letter 's' on any of his other writing.

The books had sections on the effect of ambidexterity on writing. Allen was left-handed as a child but at school he was forced to learn how to write with his right hand. The book suggested that ambidexterity had a very small effect on handwriting. The slight differences in muscular coordination between the hands meant slight changes in style but the differences were not significant. The learnt features of the handwriting remained the same.

Other chapters in the books dealt with deathbed signatures, guided hand and assisted hand signatures, as well as a person's state of health, both mental and physical, and attempts to disguise a signature. The section on deathbed signatures was of interest to me. Allen on one occasion was able to produce a close to perfect signature on one of his cheques. The letters were well formed, the spacing between the letters was even, the writing was close to horizontal above a line and the letter shapes were consistent. It still did not resemble the final Will signatures in any way but it was very similar to the signatures that he produced in his younger days. The chapter on deathbed signatures suggests that spells of writing control may return, only to be lost hours or days later. As death approaches one's ability to control a writing instrument diminishes to the point that little that is legible can be executed.

In the sections on guided hand and assisted hand, two scenarios were given. The first was where the writer's hand is guided through the signature by another person. The hand guider takes on the dominant role in the writing process. In this instance, the signature takes on the characteristics of the hand guider. The second is the assisted hand, where the writer controls the pen but there could be another person touching or steadying the writer. The signature takes on the characteristics of the assisted person's handwriting. I thought the former could have been possible in Allen's case but discounted the latter as unlikely.

28. Beryl Takes Control of the Assets

Beryl did not apply for probate on this 2007 Will but merely photocopied the final page showing that she was noted as the executor of the estate and presented this to people and businesses as evidence of her right to take control of Allen's assets. A Grant of Probate was a legal declaration that stated a Will was legally valid. No one questioned the validity of the document she produced. No one queried the fact that it was a photocopy of a page that was not officially certified, nor was there any evidence of probate being granted on the photocopied page of the alleged Will. I received letters from business and government authorities informing me of the executor taking control of the estate and becoming the recipient of all future correspondence on behalf of the estate. The local council sent me the rate notice for the farm. A week later the council sent me a copy of Beryl's letter declaring her claim to be the estate's executor and requested that I return the rate notice, as I did not have a right to be in possession of it. I telephoned the Council about their letter. I asked the person from the rates department why they thought that Beryl was the proper representative for the estate and I was told that she is noted as the executor in the will. I stated that she was NOT the executor as the estate is going through a litigation and there is no legally appointed executor. The council representative said, 'We have a copy of Mr. Johnson's Will where it clearly states that Beryl Bilk is the executor.' I asked him whether the Will copy that he has bears an official stamp from the probate office. He replied, 'No.' I told him that it is not a legal document and the council cannot abide by it. He stated emphatically, 'This is the document that we were given and we believe it is genuine.' 'It is not our job to question its legality we have to follow her directions.' I was flabbergasted by his statement. I said to him, 'How about if I showed the council a similar document with a more recent date on it stating that I was the executor would they also acknowledge it as a legal will. He replied, 'Yes, if I convinced them that it was genuine.' I rang the banks and talked to representatives there and received a similar response. I was shocked by these statements. It seems any person can write up their own documents and no one questions whether they are genuine or honest. I was so incensed I felt like making my own Will dated a day later than Beryl's Will with me as the executor and taking it to the same places to really confuse things but I did not because it would not be legal and it would affect my credibility if and when we went to court.

It was obvious to me that I was being cheated out of my entitlement. I was angry that Beryl felt that she could take was not really hers without going through the proper legal process. I needed a lawyer who specialized in Wills. My lawyer introduced me to Thomas White-Knight, and I engaged his services to handle my case.

At my first meeting with Thomas, after he had listened to my story and read through the Will, he told me that there were a lot of problems with the Will, the first being the clause that ensured that I would not get anything from the estate. He asked me whether Allen had informed me that he was writing a Will that had such a clause in it. I told him, "No." He told me that a Will maker cannot impose a condition on a beneficiary in a Will without telling the person about it, as the person has no way of knowing that they need to comply with a condition. It was a Hollywood movie scenario but not something that could apply in a real life situation because if the Will maker died an hour later or within days of signing the Will, the condition-imposed person has no way of being able to attempt to comply with the condition. This also meant that the Will maker was effectively giving that beneficiary nothing because he/she could die before the beneficiary had a chance to meet the condition. This is what happened in my situation.

In addition to this, there were many tradecraft errors in the Will that gave him the impression that a trained professional did not write it. He refrained from commenting about my claims over the signature discrepancies and suggested that the focus be made on the deficiencies in the actual Will and the fact that I had been left nothing when as a domestic partner Allen had a legal responsibility to provide for me. The claims that I was going to make against Grant of Probate being made on the Will were the fact that Allen lacked testamentary capacity (he did not have the mental cognition to know what he was doing) at the time of the Will being made and he lacked knowledge and approval of it. The issue of him failing to make provision for me in it would be handled by Oona Macafferty.

The first course of action was for Thomas to put a caveat on the grant of probate for the Will so that the probate office would know that legal action was planned. Then he had to contact the lawyer who allegedly made the Will, Neville McNaughton, who was also now in charge of handling the de-facto case on behalf of the estate. He needed to know the background information relevant to the making and signing of the Will and he wanted copies of the lawyer's Will making files. He did not have any success with Neville, who refused to comment on any of the matters raised in relation to the making of the final Will. There was also a problem with this legal firm handling the case for the Wayne and Beryl as Neville was an important witness to the making of the final Will and acting for them in a legal capacity, defending the case on their behalf.

My lawyer wrote to the Dauntons requesting a meeting with them to discuss the circumstances leading to the signing of the Will. An offer of payment for them to have legal representation present and reimbursement for their time was made. They ignored the letters and at no time did they ever respond to any further requests for information about the signing. It seemed very odd to me that these people did not want to help their friends to convince my lawyer of the authenticity of such an important document.

After I started my Will proceedings peace seemed to reign back on the farms. As directed by Thomas I continued running them as before. I put a bull in with the cows to get them in calf again, finalised Allen's taxation bookwork to the date of his death, and arranged with various companies to send his bills directly to Beryl's address instead of mine. I sent documents and mail on to her but I never got any response. I was ignored. I did not hear anything from them or what their intentions were. Liking the solitude that I was left with, I spent a lot of my time in the house at the other farm. It was in a decrepit state and smelt terribly because of the possums that lived in the roof but I felt close to the healthy Allen there.

I seriously missed that Allen. In my own house, my memories were of him when he was sick, this house held the memories of our fun times. It was 'The Healthy Allen House'. I often went inside the house and lay on his bed, remembering the times when we slept in it together. It was a large, rambling old timber farmhouse and was stinking hot in the summer and freezing cold in the winter. Its ceilings were stained from possum urine from all the years that they lived above. When we were together in the bed I would stare at the stains and try to visualize familiar shapes in the pattern they made. There was an elephant, quite a few snakes, and birds. I revisited my shape memories while I lay there. The rest of the house did not interest me as much as the bedroom. When a person is young he/she does not realize how transient life and good health can be. People need to enjoy life to the maximum every day. I thought about May's words, "You should do what you enjoy doing now because it is too late after you are dead. Dead is forever!" I heeded these words. I left my son and daughter-in-law in charge of the farms and went on a holiday to Ecuador and the Galapagos Islands-six weeks of heaven! For a short time, I could forget my troubles and feel completely safe!

I returned all too soon. I now had two legal firms acting for me, the de-facto case lawyers with Oona and the Will case lawyers with Thomas. It was going to be an expensive battle. Every month I received a bill for the previous month's legal work. Most of my wages was being spent on legal costs. I was constantly worried about how I was going to manage financially. For the first six months or so both sets of lawyers were ignored by Beryl and Wayne and their legal representatives. There were several court direction hearings where Neville McNaughton attended on behalf of them, but there was no progress in the case. Court directions and orders were ignored although Neville stated that they were in the process of applying for probate on the final Will and that is how matters remained until September. The peace did not last for long!

Beryl and Wayne started taking over the estate in earnest. It became apparent that there were visitors coming to the properties while I was at work. My neighbour Cameron would call in and let me know when he saw that I'd arrived home. He would tell me, "He was here again!" or "They were driving around the place today. She was here on her own today. They were snooping around your house today." When I went around the farms I would find that the cows were moved from the paddock that they had been in to another paddock. The gates were shut to make it obvious that someone had moved them. A few days later they were moved back again to the original paddock. When I checked the water troughs they would often be empty. Checking to find out why, I would find that the tap at the water main was turned off so no water came onto the property. I found things would be moved to different locations. I was obvious that these things were being done to unsettle me. They were exerting a subtle control over the animals, the property and me. I expected to find the cows all missing but I was assured by my lawyers and the police that I could have them charged with theft if they moved them off the property.

Since Allen's death I had removed the exit button for my electrically operated front gate. On many occasions, the closing latch was bent out of shape and it had been forced open. I could fix it but it would be bent again on another day. It was all very surreptitious and it gave me the impression that I was being stalked I wondered what other underhand things may have been done in my absence that I did not know about. Always mindful of the wheel nuts coming loose on the tractor, I had to be constantly vigilant. Every morning before I left for work I gave the wheel nuts on my car a quick check to make sure they were still tight and on my way down the drive I tested the brakes. It made me wonder what other things I needed to be vigilant about. What was I missing?

Often at night the sensor lights around the perimeter of the house would turn on. Occasionally a nocturnal animal such as an owl flying by would cause the light to come on. However, on some nights the lights came on many times. This never happened before, it was as if someone was prowling around outside. Sometimes the security cameras would pick up movement but the picture that came up on my television screen showed nothing. The cameras were set to not sense objects closer than a metre above the ground, so possums or stray foxes would not turn them on. There was a short delay between the sensor being activated by a movement and the camera picking up a picture, so a person could walk past quickly and not show up on the screen. It was distressing for me to realize that someone could be skulking around my home while I was inside. I was constantly fearful of the unknown, 'WHAT WAS OUT THERE?' Was it someone who wanted to harm me? My death would be very convenient for the Bilks. I had prepared myself in case someone broke into the house. The passageway that led to my bedroom door was blocked by the vacuum cleaner with its associated cables and hoses to trip up any intruder. Throughout the house I had placed similar hazards so I would have some sort of warning when someone tried to sneak inside. I had a couple of very sharp, pointy-tipped knives strategically placed near my bed.

    I knew that I would not be able to fight a man but I had a plan. My knives were not large, as I could easily be disarmed and a potential attacker would be able to use such weapons against me to harm me. They were short, fine-bladed, very sharp knives, the handles of which fitted inside the palm of my hand and the blade protruded about 6cm out from my closed fist. An attacker would not be able to easily get such a knife out of my clenched fist even if the person realised that I had a knife in my hand.

    My plan was two quick stabs into the eyes, which would render an assailant incapable of seeing me while I ran away as fast as possible. Something hitting you in the eye tends to cause an instant hand to eye response, so an eye stabbing would take care of an assailant's hands, preventing a counter attack. At the time, I didn't think of buying some capsicum spray, which would have the same effect. I was not always thinking rationally and I already owned the knives. Fortunately, I never had to implement my defence plan. No one entered my house while I was there. Outside the house surrounding it I had obstacles scattered. Garden hoses scrap timber lawn mowers and similar machinery. All were tripping hazards but there were no tools. I didn't want anyone to have a handy weapon to use on me. One afternoon when I arrived home from work I found my surveillance cameras broken. I gave up on the idea of cameras and didn't replace them. It was like my electronic gate: if someone was determined to get in, there was no way of stopping them.

It merely gave them another opportunity to cost me money and exert blatant control over me and the properties.

29. Notes from My Diary

In early October Wayne and Beryl visited the farms. They had plotted more brazen harassments to inflict upon me. Cameron, the share farmer next door, saw someone entering my property and he assumed it was them. They called in at Cameron's house and offered him my farm to lease for his dairy cows to graze. They told him they only wanted minimal rent. Wayne gave Cameron his business card with his contact details.

The next day Wayne rang the property owner who lived next door to Cameron and asked him to get his business card off Cameron and to mail it back to him.

13th Friday (Unlucky for one cow!) When I arrived home from work I received a telephone call from a neighbour. He told me that Beryl had been at the farm over the road during the day. He met her waiting by the front gate and chatted to her, and she told him that she was waiting for a mobile butcher to come, as there was a sick cow on the place. She told him that the vet had been and he told her the cow had grass tetany and treated the cow for that. Grass tetany is a problem that cows get mainly due to a deficiency in magnesium, but there can be multiple causes. This cow was two years old and not a highly likely candidate to have this problem. It was suggested to her that the meat from a cow treated for grass tetany would not be too good to eat. Later in the afternoon he saw her again and she said that the cow could have had a broken back, as there was a bull living with the cows and he could have tried to mate with the cow and broken her back. She felt if it had a broken back it had to be destroyed, and it would be a shame to waste the meat.

They had a mobile butcher kill the cow and cut up the meat. If the cow had genuinely been sick for either reason, the meat would not have been particularly edible anyway. It would have been too bruised. The cow, in fact, had been mine, as I had bred it on the farm. Its mother was a cow that I owned outright. It is difficult for me to describe my feeling of desolation over the loss of this animal. I was very attached to that cow. It was so friendly that it often came up to me for a pat when I was walking around the farm. Although I was very upset over the loss there was no point seeking sympathy from anyone because it was a cow no-one cared about her but me. I realised that I lost her because she was so friendly. She would have been an easy target standing there in front of someone with a gun thinking it was a friend, not knowing that her life was in danger. I rang Beryl to have it out with her about the cow. I also wanted to know what she was doing about finalising the court case and the estate. Beryl refused to talk. She hung up the telephone as soon as she heard my voice.

Virtually every day over the next few weeks someone would be on the other farm moving the cows from one paddock to another and shutting the gates, preventing them from getting back to where they were on one day and moving them back the other way on the next day. It seemed to me that it was a ploy to unsettle me and make me lose control of my temper and do something in retaliation. Disappointingly for them I did nothing.

One Friday in late September I received a call from a local real estate agent who had been a close friend of Allen's. He informed me that he was contacted by another real estate agent who asked him if he knew of anyone who would like to buy a farm such as my place. Wayne had contacted the estate agent and told him that the property was for sale. I felt extremely unsettled upon being told this. I knew that Wayne would not have a problem with falsely attempting to claim my legal action was settled to remove the caveats so that he could arrange sale documents to transfer property ownership out of the estate. I realized that their intention was to make me feel insecure and it was working for them. I immediately checked the property title on the government website. In addition, I paid a fee so that I would be instantly notified of any change in the title details. I felt a little calmer after I had done this.

By the end of October, the scare tactics increased. Every day it was obvious that someone had been on the other farm moving the cows from one paddock to another and shutting the gates, preventing them from returning to where they were previously. The water main was also turned off, so the animals had no water. There are no windmills on that farm. Town water is the only source of water for the stock that is kept on there. It is a horrifying feeling knowing that things are being done behind my back and not being able to retaliate, have any protection or obtain any justice. A fear of the unknown is the worst fear because you cannot prepare yourself for something that you don't know will happen. It was late October and the estate was at a stage now where Beryl and Wayne had to apply for probate soon or I could apply to the court to have probate granted so the case could progress. They appointed a new law firm to act for them, Tibor Norwich and Partners. Tibor Norwich was like a new broom for the case. He wrote letters to Macafferty and Co with the intention of negotiating a settlement. Oona replied with my terms of settlement. I wanted what was left to me in Allen's penultimate Will but the matter stagnated from there. No reply was ever received from Tibor Norwich. It appeared to me that it was a set-up to indicate to the courts that they made an attempt to negotiate a settlement with me. There was to be a directions hearing the next day. This was when my lawyers were going to try to get probate granted.

Tibor Norwich requested an extension of time to prepare the case, as the firm did not have all the details of the case. They had just taken over from the previous firm and they needed time to review all the evidence. My lawyers were obliged to grant them an extension of time. Tibor Norwich applied to the court for a sixty-day adjournment of the directions hearing. The date was 27 October, which meant that the extension would be in effect until the end of December. Nothing would happen until the New Year. There would be no probate application made and the whole case would sit in abeyance for the time being.

In early November Beryl rang a neighbour, saying that she wanted to cut the grass on the farm to make some hay. She wanted to know who Allen contracted to do this. The neighbour gave her the number of the person. He was the same person that I used. I realised that she had a plan to ingratiate herself with this person by ringing him up asking for farming advice and trying to become friends with him. Later she tried to get this person to make an affidavit in her favour and denigrating me for the Will case but he chose to not take sides. He told her that he did not socialise with Allen and his association was strictly a business arrangement, so he would not be able to write anything that would be of benefit to her.

The next week Beryl was on the other farm. She cut and took my padlock that I had on the gate near the cattle stockyards. I was standing near my front gate when I saw her driving down the road to the gate on the other farm. She got out of her car with bolt cutters in her hands, went to the gate, returned to her car and left. I discovered the padlock and chain missing when I went over to check later in the day. It was there earlier in the morning, as I had been over checking the stock that morning. The police told me that it is a criminal offence for someone to cut a padlock and chain of another person's gate but in this instance, they felt that they were not able to act as the estate did not have a legal representative. Beryl returned and met with the hay making contractor later that day and instructed him to cut the grass in the paddocks for hay. She told him that there was no padlock on the gate so he could enter the property whenever he was ready. She told him to send the account to the Estate of A D Johnson at her address in Brighton.

On the following week, I was away for two nights staying with a work colleague in the city. I was teaching in the city for the week. While I was away from my home the office at my work received a call from the RSPCA saying that they needed to contact me urgently because I had a sick foal on the farm. I rang the contact number that the caller had left. The man told me that he had received a call from someone who had told him that there was a horse with a broken leg at my place. I felt frantic because I was trapped at work and I did not know what was happening to my animals at home. He said that he had been out to the property to attend to it but could not find it. I told him how many horses were on the property and he agreed that was the number of horses that he had counted. The only horse that it could have been was a foal that had a bad limp but he could not get near it or any of the horses to check it. He decided that the leg was obviously not broken by the way that it could gallop away from him, but it needed to be looked at. My horses had developed a fear of men that they didn't previously have, so the man had no chance of getting anywhere near them. They only trusted women. I had to rush home and get a vet to check the foal. It did not have anything broken but it was limping. We could not find anything that could be causing it to limp and we thought it could have been kicked by another horse but we could not find any kick marks on it. It was put it on painkillers for a week and it recovered. I never found out why it was limping in the first place.

November 13th Sunday (It wasn't a Friday but it was unlucky 13th for another cow.) Wayne and Beryl were on the other farm interfering with the cattle. I saw them and drove my car down to see what they were doing. I saw that they were about to castrate a bull calf of mine and I protested that I wanted it left as a bull. They declared that it was going to be done and I had no say in the matter. Wayne then started swearing at me and yelled abuse at me, criticising my care of the animals and the fact that I had not castrated the animal when it was a calf. He swore at me again then he told me, "This is cruelty to animals. It should have been castrated as a calf. We don't want any bulls on the place!" I was seething because it was a very well-bred animal and was most suitable to be kept as a bull.

I told them that the cows belonged to me and they said, "Why haven't you taken them away?" I wanted to tell them that I was waiting for an outcome to the legal proceedings but I thought in the circumstances it would be better for me to stay silent. While they were there I rang the police, and explained the situation. The police asked, "Who is the executor of the estate? Who has probate on the Will?" I explained that probate had not been applied for yet. The police told me that there was not much that they could do. As there was no appointed executor, if Wayne and Beryl felt that they had a right to enter the property and castrate a calf then there was nothing that the police could do. I would have to apply to the courts to have the situation changed. That, of course, would be much too late for the bull. His balls were going for good in ten minutes.

While I was talking to the police Beryl became agitated and started yelling at me so I took out my camera and started filming her swearing. Wayne got very angry and ran over to his car to get something. I became extremely apprehensive, I already had the car engine running, so I changed gear and put the car into drive to get away quickly if the situation made it necessary. I knew that Wayne kept a gun in his car. Fortunately, he only pulled out his camera and started filming me filming them. I burst out laughing at the ludicrousness of it all and because there was nothing else that I could do anyway. I didn't know whether they intended to do anything else with the cattle so I sat in my car on the street and filmed them until they let the cattle go. I decided to go over to a neighbour's place to stay with them for a while until they left.

The next day I moved all my cows to the farm where I lived. I considered that I was told to move them so I did. I also contacted my lawyers to get advice on what I could do in the situation and they told me that the courts would consider the matter trivial and not look at me very favourably for wasting valuable court time on such a minor matter. There was not much that I could do about things. The best that they could do was to send a stern warning letter to their lawyer. I was stuck because they were ignoring court directions and not applying for probate.

December 22nd, 2007 There was an east-west freeway extension being built north of my place. This freeway cut a north-south running road in half, which meant that property owners south of the new freeway needed another road so that they could leave their properties. The northern boundary of my farm had a section of government land along it that was reserved for a future road. This land was disused and overgrown with gorse bushes so no cars could drive down it. I loved having it there, as I had my own private bush horse riding area off the farm where there were no cars. I had an access gate halfway along the side boundary of the property so that I could enter and leave the property without riding on the road where there was traffic. Because of the freeway that road reserve was made into a proper road for the property owners that lived between my place and the new freeway. The gate into my farm was still there but I had a padlock on it to prevent casual passers-by from entering my property or opening the gate and leaving it open so the animals could escape.

Early one morning I heard large cattle transport trucks driving down the new road, and it sounded like they had stopped somewhere in the vicinity of my side gate. I could hear a lot of cows mooing and the noise of cows stamping around in a truck. I went outside to have a look and sure enough, there were cows being jumped off the trucks onto the road and herded into my paddock through the gate. I drove my car to where the trucks were stopped. I saw my padlock cut in two and lying on the ground. Then I saw Wayne herding the cows off the truck and through the gate into the paddock. I was very nervous when I saw him; however, there was a truck driver sitting in the cabin of his truck. He was watching Wayne but not doing anything to help him so I concluded that he was only being paid to transport the cows and wasn't a friend.

I felt that I would not be in danger with the driver being there so I confronted Wayne. He told me that the cows belonged to his wife and he was putting them there because he could not feed them. I advised him that he needed to put his cows on the other farm, as it had a town water supply connected. This farm only had water bores pumped by windmills. They would not be able to pump enough water for all the stock on the farm. How did he intend to get them water? He said, "Let me worry about that. It is none of your business." I informed him that he was not supposed to be putting his cows on the farm anyway, as I was in possession of the property and my de-facto proceedings had not been resolved yet. He bellowed at me, "It will be ten years before that happens. All those letters that your lawyers have sent us, they mean nothing to us. NOTHING! You had best leave before there is real trouble (I considered that he was threatening me)." As I was leaving he shouted after me, "We have to do these things to you because of what you did to Allen. You hounded him taking out your de-facto proceedings. WE HAVE TO PUNISH YOU!"

All of Wayne and Beryl's cows had large yellow plastic tags pierced through their ears with the word BILK written on them. The tags looked like earrings and they clearly identified the cows as belonging to them. They were in a severely emaciated condition and very weak from starvation. Some of them had an extremely painful and contagious eye disease called pink eye. Treatment for this condition is very simple but it was obvious that none of the cows had received any treatment to ease their suffering. Two of their cows were in a very bad way and were not able to walk. Wayne left them lying on the ground without any attention. Four cows escaped down the road and broke the neighbour's fences. They were left in that paddock. Another two truckloads of cattle were left on the other farm. They were locked in a paddock without any water.

These sick and dying cows were left dumped on me with very little food or water. They did not care about the welfare of their animals. I could not walk out in the paddock where the cows were because they charged at me. They behaved like wild bulls, pawing at the ground, snorting and charging. I barely managed to run to the nearest fence and climb through it to evade one of the crazed cows. I rang the police because Wayne threatened me and I didn't know what I could do in the situation. The police officer that I spoke with said that it sounded to him like I was being stalked. He told me to go to the police station and pick up some information on stalking. He recommended that I should take out an intervention order against them. He also said that the courts were closed for Christmas from that day until mid-January so there was little that I could do in the interim.

Wayne and Beryl certainly had planned this! I rang Thomas White-Knight and he contacted their lawyer, Tibor Norwich, who was very obstinate. A letter of objection was sent to Tibor Norwich pointing out that their cows were wild and dangerous. If I, my friends or anyone in my family was hurt by their cows they would face litigation. They were also informed that I could not be held responsible for the welfare of their animals. There was a notation made informing them of the sick and injured animals that required urgent veterinary attention but it was ignored. They did not have any empathy for the suffering that their stock was forced to endure. Thomas also told me to put padlocks on the internal gates on the property to keep my cows separate from theirs.

The next day One of the sick cows on the ground was able to get up and walk away but the other was still unable to get up. Their cows were very wild and dangerous so I could not go near them. A person from the RSPCA contacted me about the sick cow. A neighbour had seen it lying on the ground and called them. I instructed them to contact Wayne and Beryl.

On Christmas Eve morning, there was no wind and the troughs connected to the first windmill on my property were out of water; also, the tank that the windmill pumped the water into was empty. I contacted the RSPCA on Sunday morning and told them about the cows being out of water and of my concern about this.

Wayne and Beryl came late Sunday morning and were on the farm for some hours. They entered the property by the side road gate along the north side of the property. This is the same gate that they used to deliver the cattle on Friday. They did not come near the house. They attended to the sick cow but it was still lying on the ground when they left. They somehow got it into the middle of the paddock, hidden among some bushes so that it could not be seen from the road. The cow died the next day. They spent some time down the paddock near the windmill. They drove down the back of the farm where my cattle were grazing. There is a fence at the windmill separating the front section of the farm from the back section, and there are two gates. As I had been instructed by my lawyer, both gates now had padlocks and chains on them to keep my cattle from becoming mixed up with theirs. They cut off my padlocks and stole my chains. They then put their cows down the back section of the farm with my cows.

I often fed my cows on apple pulp that I got from a local apple juicing factory. My cows loved the apple pulp and they would come running to me if I called them, expecting to be fed something nice. Their cows were wild and they ran away when they saw people. After they left the property I went down to the very back paddock and called to my cows. They ran to me and I shut them in that paddock. Their cows ran the other way, away from me towards the front of the farm. When they were in the front paddock I shut the gate and trapped them there. I had my cows separated from theirs and both lots of cows were back in the paddocks where they were before.

Within minutes of me finishing this job Beryl and Wayne returned and chased their cows towards the back of the farm to mix them with my cows again. They then removed the gates completely and took them away. They spent the next hour driving back and forth along the road watching me. I was not brave enough to go out to move the cows again. I telephoned my son and daughter–in-law and they came out and helped me to separate the cows again. While we were doing this, they drove their car up and down the street at high speed, sounding the car horn, yelling, swearing and screaming denigrating statements at me and my family. They did not enter the property while my family was there. I removed a couple of gates from another paddock near my house and replaced the missing gates so the two herds of cows could remain separated. A couple of hours later my family left, thinking they would have gone to their home by then.

Not a chance of that! They were covertly sitting waiting to invade again. About twenty minutes later I saw them back on the property. They drove down to the windmill fence and started to ram their car at high speed into the fence posts, smashing them out of the ground. They dragged the wires across the paddock with their car. I tried to film them but they were too far away for my camera to show identifying pictures. They seemed to be in a raging mood and I was not going to risk going closer. Later, after they had thoroughly smashed the fences and gates with their car, they started chasing the cows with their car. They first started chasing my cows toward the front of the farm where their own cows were. They were driving so fast that clouds of dust were rising behind the car. I could see them hitting my cows with their car if the cows did not move fast enough. When the two herds of cows were together they chased them down the back of the farm again. They drove at a furious speed for a rough paddock sounding the car horn while yelling and screaming.

I rang the police, knowing that they could do very little. The officer that I spoke with yelled out to her colleagues in the background, "It's her again! They're at it again!" By this time my family had arrived back and Wayne and Beryl, on seeing this, left the property. This was after having done considerable damage to the fences and exhausting the cows. It was getting dark and I did not venture down the paddock that night; I decided to leave well enough alone. We could not see much and I was worried about the effect the chasing was having on the cows. They needed a rest.

The next morning, I inspected the damage. I found one of my cows dead and a few were limping very badly. They seemed to be able to walk okay so it appeared that there were no broken bones; they probably had bad bruising. The fences were badly smashed and the wires were cut up or mangled on the ground. I could not get my injured cows into the cattle yards to do anything with them. They were too distressed and kept running away with the wild cows. They eventually got better but it took a few weeks. I rang a local fencing contractor and told him what had happened. He came to my place that day and repaired my fences. This time I didn't put in wooden posts. He had sections of steel railway line that he used for posts instead. If they tried to ram these with their car it would do some serious damage to their car before these posts would break. After the fences were fixed I got some apple pulp from the orchard for my cows so I could separate the two lots again. My cows, on seeing the apple-filled trailer, chased it down the paddock. The wild cows had never eaten apple so they ignored the trailer and car. I kept my fingers crossed that my cows would be fine.

Peace reigned on the farms during Christmas Day but that was a transient reprieve the war resumed in full force on the next day! Wayne was driving around the farm alone (I felt very jittery and nervous about him being there while I was in the house alone). One of their cows had died. He dragged the dead cow's carcass to the gateway for the knackery man to take away. I did not see them on the farm on Thursday, Friday or Saturday, but I noticed that another gate had been removed from the property. It was there on Tuesday 26th. After this I was left in peace until New Year's Eve. They did not seem to worry whether their cows had water or not. As the property occupier I was left with the responsibility of ensuring that there was sufficient water for them to drink. This was a problem, as the only available water was pumped by the windmill, and that required wind to operate it. It was the middle of summer. The cows drank a lot of water because it was hot and there was not a lot of wind to turn the windmill. Somehow the windmill seemed to have sufficient wind to pump enough water in the evenings. The cows soon drank this and they had to wait all day without a drink, until the next evening for the windmill to pump more water for them to drink.

They returned on the morning of New Year's Eve. They smashed the gates at the windmill and mixed up the cows again. This time they left the fence alone. I was telling my neighbours about what they were doing and one neighbour offered his place for me to put my cows on for a couple of weeks to help me save their lives until I could get an intervention order from the courts. My family came and helped me to move my cows to the neighbour's property. We put their cows into the only paddock where we could contain them (that was a paddock that still had a gate), while we moved my cows. To move the cows, I took them down the back of the farm and through an adjoining gate into one neighbour's farm. We had to go across that farm to get to the farm where I wanted to leave them. Wayne and Beryl came onto my farm while I was moving my cows, took the gate away and chased their cows down to the back of the farm.

Fortunately, I had got my cows off the property and they were being moved across the neighbour's property by that time, so both herds of cattle did not get mixed together. Beryl and Wayne knew exactly what they could get away with legally, so they did not dare to enter the neighbour's property. I walked the cows across the back of one farm along a creek at the back boundary to the next neighbour's farm. This was very easy because I had more apple pulp in a trailer. The cows followed the trailer as if they had been trained to do it. While I was moving my cows, they were in their car on my place and drove at breakneck speed up and back alongside the fence that separated the neighbour's place from mine while yelling the usual obscenities of course. My neighbours had visitors for a New Year party and everyone could hear them yelling in my direction. They were shocked! They could not believe that those people would say such things and behave like that.

Later in the afternoon (about 4pm) I drove the tractor down the road with some hay to the paddock where I had my cows to feed them. My son followed me in his car. They appeared again and chased my son down the road in their car. Luke kept his vehicle in the centre of the road so that they could not pass him to harass me on the tractor. The neighbour who owned the property where I put the cows and his guests all watched them driving down the road. They called the police and told them to come out. I was feeling very intimidated by their presence. I felt that they had no right to do what they were doing because I was not interfering with their cows and what I was doing was none of their business. My son talked with the police when they arrived, as I was still with the cows. They had driven off before the police got there, driving down the road in the opposite direction from the way the police came. I felt that they must have had someone watching up the street to warn them of the arrival of any police.

During the next couple of weeks, I was under so much stress that I was at breaking point. I did not feel at all safe when they were prowling on the property. I was afraid to go outside to do anything while they were there. I would watch out for them to leave before I ventured out of the house but they would return as if they had been watching and waiting for me to do this. Sometimes I would wait for a few hours but they still turned up. I liked to go for a walk around the farm every evening rather than drive the car. Now whenever I went walking it was always at the time when my dairy farmer neighbour was out in the adjacent paddock herding his cows in for milking, and I walked alongside the dividing fence so that I could climb over the fence into the neighbour's place in an emergency. I always tried to get a neighbour or my son to be present when I wanted to do any work outside.

With my cattle on the neighbour's property I could look after them in safety, but I still had my horses to care for. Wayne and Beryl drove up and down the road beside the property, making me feel intimidated. They did not enter the property when I had another person with me but I still felt frightened and shaky. I felt stressed all the time, even when I was inside the house. I was so frightened about using the tractor, because of what happened to the wheel nuts, that I now left it hidden at a neighbour's. I was constantly worried about what they would do to me next.

On New Year's Day Beryl was going around the property alone. My neighbour and I watched her behaving as if she owned the place. I did not go near her because I thought it might be a trap to try to provoke me into having an argument with her allowing Wayne to appear and take retaliatory action.

I did not see either of them over the next two days but I saw fresh tyre tracks in the dirt. Evidence left to ensure I was aware that I was not getting any peace. I went out during the day so they must have been on the property during my absence.

On Thursday January 4th Wayne came out and drove over the property. I felt sure that he was trying to provoke me because he was there for hours driving around and around back and forth from the front of the farm to the back again and again.

I thought back to the times when Wayne would come to the farm and visit with Allen and May. He loved telling them how smart he was in his business dealings. "He always had to win," Allen would tell me. "If he thinks he is losing, he goes harder." I remembered one conversation that I was a party to where Allen was concerned about a change in the landlord tenancy laws. He was worried how it would affect him with his flats and the rental income that he received from them if he had a problem tenant. Wayne boasted to him, "I don't worry about things like that. If I have a tenant that I want to get rid of I'll pitch a tent in their front yard and camp there. I will annoy them so much that they will get sick of me and pack up and leave." He didn't put up a tent on my place but he dumped cows on me and now he got to annoy me by hanging around and interfering with my animals. He did not consider that it was illegal to harass people even if he thought he had a right to do as he pleased with his late father-in-law's property.

My mother, who lived in Queensland, came down to stay with me. This made me feel safer at night, having another person in the house. My mother would watch them driving back and forth in their car and she would state, "If they want to waste all of their holidays driving around like that, let them! We will stay inside where it is comfortable and cool." My mother is not fond of animals and did not care what happened to them.

30. Getting Court Protection

JANUARY 8TH, it was the New Year 2008 and the courts were open. I filed for intervention orders against Beryl and Wayne Bilk and attended the court where an interim intervention order was issued. I brought my cows home from the neighbours because there was no more grass for them to eat there and it was costing me too much to feed them.

The next day the Bilks, as I now thought of them, intended to go out with a BANG! I saw them entering the property and they drove down the back. I could see them tearing around the paddocks in their car breaking the fences and gates again! I wondered 'Why did I waste my money fixing them?' I rang the police and they told me that the intervention order had not been served on them yet but they knew that the order existed and that they were going to be served. The police came straight out with the intention of serving the orders on them while they were on the property but they got away before the police arrived. The police and I drove down to the back of the farm and checked the damage. Fences were smashed; wires were cut and mangled. Gates were removed and the metal fittings in the fence posts to hold the gates were broken off so that I could not put replacement gates onto the posts. While we were down there looking at the fences one of my cows lay on the ground and died right before our eyes. It was a young cow, and it had seemed quite healthy to me up until then. I was devastated and could not stop myself from crying which made the police cry as well. At least they showed some empathy for my animals.

> The intervention order was served on them later that day. The orders stated that they were prohibited from:
>
> 1. Stalking, assaulting, harassing, threatening or intimidating the victim of stalking.
>
> 2. Approaching, telephoning or contacting the victim of stalking except to participate in mediation by agreement with the victim of stalking.
>
> 3. Knowingly being at or within 1000 metres of the premises.

4. Damaging property owned/jointly owned by the victim of stalking.

5. Causing another person to engage in conduct prohibited by this order.

6. Possessing, carrying or using any firearm; any firearms licence, permit or authority is suspended and the defendant is to surrender any firearm and licence, permit or authority immediately to a member of the police force.

Wayne kept a licenced gun in his car and the police took this off him.

Two days after the order had been served Beryl turned up and drove over the property while I was out walking around it. It seemed to me that she did not consider the court order applied to her. I felt enraged that she presumed she could blatantly do as she pleased with no consequences. She was brazenly in breach of the intervention order so I called the police but she got away before they arrived. She must have had someone watching out for the police to turn down the road so that she could be warned.

A further hearing was scheduled for 17th January where the Bilks could attend to argue their case. Their lawyer stated that for their defence they would have witnesses to appear on their behalf, including the vet who they alleged attended the cow that they had slaughtered and the mobile butcher who actually slaughtered the cow. The truck driver who transported the cows to my place was to be there, and various other people who would be witnesses on their behalf.

They did not attend the hearing. Not one of their intended witnesses appeared either. Their lawyer and barrister were the only people who appeared to represent them. Their legal representatives misled the judge, claiming that the probate application had been advertised and applied for on Allen's Will. They falsely claimed that Beryl was the executrix of the estate. A check with the probate office later that day proved that no application for probate had been made by her. Her legal representatives lied presumably under Beryl's direction. I felt sure that they would do a lot more lying before this was over.

When someone intends applying for probate on a Will, that person must place an advertisement in a newspaper stating the fact. That gives anyone who may feel that they are owed money by the deceased person an opportunity to make a claim against the estate. My lawyer could not find any advertisement in any newspaper to indicate that she intended to apply for probate. In court, their barrister tried to argue that his clients were not stalking me, they were only on the property to care for their cows, but the judge did not agree. The Interim Intervention order stayed in force. The one concession that the judge gave them was the 1000 metre separation distance was reduced to 200 metres. Their barrister tried to get the judge to permit Wayne to have his gun back but the judge would not allow it.

On the Australia Day holiday 26th January, the Bilks had another dead cow. They got a man who was working down the road with an excavator to bury the carcass. When they were leaving they drove down the side road. I was outside and saw them stop by the paddock fence where I had my horses. I had a new-born foal that was sleeping beside the fence near where they stopped. They got out of their car and threw things at it to frighten it. It woke with a start, jumped up and ran away squealing. I was sure they did it because they saw me watching them and wanted to be nasty. After they had left I went over to check that the foal was not injured and discovered about a dozen large rocks on the ground where the foal had been lying down. Fortunately, the foal appeared to be okay. I was back at work now and I did not see them again for a few days.

31. I Get a Flat Car Tyre. And Again! And Again! And Again...!

It was early in the morning and I was leaving for work. I got into my car and drove out of my garage but something was wrong with the car. There was an unusual noise. A bump, bump, bump sound was coming from underneath the car. I felt chills come over me. Oh! No! I forgot to check the wheel nuts! I stopped and got out and walked around my car checking the wheels. My back tyre was flat! I had to change it as I am quite capable of changing my own tyre and keep a pair of gardening gloves along with a light coverall in the back of the car for such emergencies. After donning my tyre-changing outfit I set to work. Fifteen minutes later I was back at the wheel and under way again. I drove down the road and onto the highway when I started having a problem with steering the car. What is wrong now? I thought as I stopped the car on the side of the road, got out, and walked around to have a look. I had another flat tyre! It wasn't completely flat so I decided to add some more air to it and try to drive to a repair shop. I had a small air compressor in my car that operated from my cigarette lighter which I kept it in my car to inflate basketballs at work. I taught sport and the school had many inflatable balls that always seemed to go flat during the lessons. My car was parked beside the sport playing area so that it was convenient to pump up the balls using the battery-operated compressor rather than using a hand operated ball pump.

I used my compressor to add some air to the tyre and hoped it would remain sufficiently inflated to get to the nearest tyre repair facility that was about five kilometres away. Not having another spare tyre, I didn't have much of an option. Although I made it I had to wait twenty minutes for the shop to open. I suffered the stress of knowing I would be late for work that day but at least I was still alive so I would eventually get there.

When the tyres were examined to find the cause of them being flat, each tyre had a rusty screw firmly imbedded into the tread, causing the air to leak out slowly. After the repairs were done I put the experience down to bad luck and went to work. Two days later I found that I had another flat tyre! Oh! How annoying! Another tyre change was required and another trip was made to the repairers. Bad luck again!

Three days later while I was driving along the freeway I started losing control of my steering and then the now familiar baboomp, baboomp, baboomp sound under the car started. Sure enough, I had another flat tyre! I was becoming very adept at changing tyres now. I didn't need to worry; I was stopped on the side of the freeway. A damsel in distress! No sooner had I jacked up the car and opened the boot to get the spare tyre out when help arrived. A very nice man pulled up and took over the process. He would not even let me help. We had a lovely chat and when he had finished he advised me to go straight to a tyre place and get the tyre repaired, as I didn't have a useable spare any more. I thanked him for his help and assured him that I would go straight away and get my tyre fixed. I got it fixed at a place near where I worked and managed to not be late that day. This tyre also had an old rusty screw in it.

That afternoon when it was time for everyone to go home after work one of my colleagues came running in, frantically screaming out "Catherine, Catherine, you have a flat tyre! Quick, quick call the RACV!" (The RACV or Royal Automobile Club of Victoria is a club that people join so that they can get assistance when they have problems with their car). "Another flat tyre?" I responded. "I can't be bothered waiting for the RACV; I'll change it myself." "You know how to change a tyre!" he exclaimed. This man was very young and knew nothing about how cars functioned. He only knew how to drive them. He followed me out and watched me change the tyre. "How do you know you are doing it right?" he asked me. "What if the wheel falls off when you drive away? What will you do?" "Don't worry," I assured him "I have done this many times before and I have never had the wheel fall off." On my way home, I got the tyre repaired. Sure enough, it had an old rusty screw embedded in the tread. This was starting to get very annoying and expensive. I began to think that the flat tyres were more than just coincidence.

When I arrived home, I examined the floor of my garage to see if there was anything lying on the concrete. No, there was nothing, nor was there anything on the ground in front of my garage. It was very puzzling. I felt perplexed. The next morning, I had another loss of steering problem while driving along the freeway and discovered that I had another flat tyre. This time a very nice man in a truck pulled up and helped me change it. Another repair was needed and another rusty screw was found. I was starting to feel very creeped out. Was someone sneaking around my house and pushing old screws into my tyres during the night? I did not know what to do. The next day was Saturday and I walked down my driveway to my front gate. On the way, I discovered hundreds of old rusty screws scattered along in the gravel. At last I had found the source of my problems! The rest of my day was spent searching for every screw, which was not an easy task. They were the same colour as the gravel and very difficult to see. I had a few magnets in the shed so I got these and tied them to some string so that I could drag them along the driveway. This was very successful. I lost track of how many screws that I found but it was more than six hundred. They had been scattered there deliberately to make my life difficult. I was very lucky that I didn't have an accident when my tyres went flat while driving down the freeway.

32. There's Something Wrong with the Water

There was no town water supply on my farm. The water for my home came from rainwater tanks attached to my house. I preferred the taste of my rainwater over the chlorinated city water but I was always conscious of having a pure supply of water. My tanks are always sealed to prevent insects such as mosquitoes getting into the water tank and laying eggs. All openings had fine gauze mesh in them and there were overflow attachments on my downpipes to collect the debris from the roof to prevent it from going into my tanks. These precautions were not enough on this particular evening when I wanted a drink of water. I filled a glass from the tap in the kitchen and as I started drinking I thought that the water had an odd smell. I swallowed my first mouthful, found that it tasted terrible and spat out most of it. The rest of the water was tipped into the sink and I went to bed. About an hour later I woke with the most excruciating stomach cramps. I was in pain for a couple of hours but then the pains passed and I went to sleep. I did not give much thought to the pain the next day and went off to work as usual.

I didn't drink any tank water that morning, I only had my usual glass of milk with my toast for breakfast. That night when I got home from work I went to take another drink of water, having forgotten about my previous day's experience. The same smell was in the water and the same taste. Again, I only swallowed a small sip before spitting the rest of the water out. While I was out walking around the cows I again had painful stomach cramps. I decided that there was a connection between the water and the pain and immediately went back to the house to inspect my water tanks. Everything looked the same with the mesh seals all intact, but on one of the mesh strainers the screws that held it in place had been removed. I had not undone the screws so who could have done it? When? I was puzzled. Lifting the strainer, I peered inside the tank and was immediately overcome by the smell of the water inside. I did not know what was causing the smell but it was not good.

I decided to undo the pipes at the bottom to empty out the tank to see if there was something dead in it. For water to use overnight I transported some new water home from the town supply connected on the other farm in a small water tank on a trailer that I kept for fire-fighting in the summer. By the next morning there was a lake of smelly water on the ground around the tank and the tank was empty. I could see nothing in the tank or the water on the ground to indicate what was causing the smell.

Before I left for work I used a high pressure washer to thoroughly clean the inside of the tank, using the water in my fire tank. Then I rang a water transporting company to get them to deliver a truckload of water to refill the tank. While I was at work that day I told people about my water problems and everyone suggested that I should have had my water tested to find out what was wrong with it. I hadn't thought of that. I had never had a problem with my water before so it was too unusual for me to be aware of doing something like that. Someone suggested that maybe my water had been poisoned!

Now I was feeling very worried, I wished I had known to test my water for contaminants. It was too late now to test my water supply because it was summertime and the water on the ground would have dried up by the time that I got home from work. I decided not to drink the water from my tanks again and only drink water bought from the supermarket. I would only use my own water for bathing and washing my clothes. I bought drinking water from the supermarket in five-litre containers. That night I went to bed thinking about my water supply and feeling very uneasy. At four am I suddenly woke up in horror. The hairs on my body were standing on end. I had goose bumps. It suddenly dawned on me! The farms are riddled with poisons. In the house over the road there were large metal containers with arsenic and many other containers with different chemicals. What if someone did want to poison me? There was a ready supply of toxic potions sitting there. I could not sleep another wink. I immediately got up, dressed and drove over to the other farm.

My first stop was the house, where I removed all the containers of chemicals that I thought could be toxic. These chemicals were made long before any form of danger labelling or warnings were used on toxic chemical containers. Most did not even list the chemicals contained in the concoction that the product was made from. The smell emitted from the containers was bad enough to give me an indication of the likelihood that the contents could be harmful. I wore rubber gloves while handling them and wished that I had some sort of protective breathing apparatus. Every smelly tin was transferred from the house to the Ute tray. When I was happy that I had removed every toxic chemical container from the house, I drove to the shearing shed. In this shed there were even more tins containing chemicals, including the nasty, ancient one, Carbon Tetrachloride, that May had told me often killed the sheep when they used it to worm them.

    I put everything into the Ute. The drums of Agent Orange; the two large heavy drums of powdered arsenic based sheep lice treatment for bathing the sheep; the container of diazinon; the Carbon tetrachloride; the Phostoxin that is used for killing rabbits. This one is deadly! Once the dried pellets get wet they give off phosphine gas that kills instantly if it is inhaled. Then it disappears from the body without leaving any detectable trace. What a way to kill someone and get away with it. Stomach cramping is one of the symptoms of Phostoxin poisoning if it is ingested. After I read this on the internet I felt horrified learning that maybe I could have been killed from drinking my water. It is not absorbed through the skin so washing clothes and bathing in Phostoxin contaminated water will not affect a person. I seriously regretted not getting my water tested but I realized that if the water was poisoned with something already on the farm there would be no way of tracing where the poison came from or who put it there anyway. These chemical containers and many others all had to go! When I arrived home, I parked the Ute well away from my house in one of the sheds. I found that the smell emanating from the chemical tins was nauseating. The whole shed was stinky. My next problem was what to do with the chemicals. I could not leave them there. I knew that there were places that farmers could take old chemicals for safe disposal, so I found the nearest collection centre on the Internet. The collection centres had set dates when farmers could deliver their chemicals for disposal, and the centres only took chemicals on these dates. The soonest collection date was two months away. I was stuck with drums of chemicals stinking out my shed for two months. Worse still, they were not locked away so any daytime farm visitor could easily tip the chemicals into my water tank or into my animals' water troughs while I was at work. My dilemma had increased massively. I had to drive to work in the Ute every day until I could find a way to dispose of the chemicals. I drove very cautiously concentrating on the road knowing that I was driving a chemical bomb. I wondered whether I should have had Hazardous Chemical warning signs on the car like the ones that truck drivers have on their trucks. 'Drive carefully!' I warned myself. 'Drive very carefully!'

I recalled advertisements that I had read in the past where collectors wanted to buy old farm memorabilia, including old oil and fuel cans as well as old farm chemical containers. I had lots of very old farm chemical containers that were in very good condition. Probably the chemicals within them were still in very good condition although quite toxic! I bought a copy of the paper that I knew often had the type of wanted advertisement that I needed. There were a few collectors advertising in that paper and I rang the first number, but the person did not want drums with the chemicals still in them. Persistence paid off, and the third person that I rang said that he was interested and he would come out and take a look the next day. When he turned up he told me that he would have preferred to not have the chemicals in the tins but he wanted the containers so he bought every tin off me and paid me twenty dollars. He said that he would have paid me a lot more money if the tins had been empty because he now had the inconvenience of disposing of the unwanted chemicals. I was happy the chemicals were immediately gone from my life, and that was all that mattered. I lived in fear every day that something was going to happen to me or my animals, I felt watched. I was now more vulnerable than I had ever been in my life.

33. The Pick Up

Early one Saturday morning in February, I went out to do some shopping. Wayne suddenly appeared in his car and followed me when I was driving down the road to the local shopping centre. He kept his car over the required 200 metre separation distance as designated in the intervention order, but I still considered that he was deliberately following me. I thought I saw another man in the car with him, but I was not sure. I was going to call the police but I lost sight of him when I parked. As I got out of my car and walked towards a computer shop to buy something, I sensed that I was being followed. It was a dark-haired man walking behind me, not Wayne. I felt okay until the man followed me into the shop. I turned around and he smiled and winked at me. I was not sure what to do in that situation, but to be polite I smiled back at him and walked out of the shop.

He followed me and caught up to me. "Excuse me, do you know where the Commonwealth Bank is around here?" he asked me. "You are standing right outside it now." I replied. We were in fact standing outside the bank. He said. "OH! I forgot. It's Saturday, it is not open today. Would you like a cup of coffee?" I didn't really want a cup of coffee with this stranger, but I was curious as to why he was following me and trying to pick me up.

He was a very attractive man about my age, of slim build with a full head of black hair and piercing blue eyes. While we sat we talked a little about him and his job, he told me that he was a property evaluator and gave me his business card. I was immediately puzzled by his business card. The card was plain white. It only had his first name on it and a mobile telephone number, followed by the words Property Evaluator. Nothing else was written on the card. One would have expected a business card to have the person's last name and some sort of business address. I thought it possibly should have had some extra information about the services he offered. He questioned me about whether I had a man in my life and also asked me where I lived and whether I had any property. I thought this was a rather long-winded process to procure some business. He asked quite a few other unusual questions. I felt that he was fishing for information rather than trying to pick me up. I told him that I did not live locally and I was only passing through. The conversation started to fizzle out from there, and I managed to thank him for the drink and get away. I still wondered why the man wanted to talk to me in the first place.

Considering I had come straight from the farm where I had been tending to my cows, I hardly looked like the catch of the century. I was wearing old Blundstone boots that had some dried mud and maybe a little dried cow dung on them, old farm jeans that had a couple of holes in the knees along with odd blobs of paint here and there, and my top was a very old, baggy pullover that had seen better days. I felt that he could not have been interested in me as a likely girlfriend prospect and he didn't suggest any further contact between us when we parted. I wondered if he had been the other man in Wayne's car and whether it was a set-up meeting by him to get information out of me. They needed to plan their defence for the case and they needed information. I was becoming quite paranoid now. I kept an eye out to see if Wayne was anywhere in sight but I did not see him anymore on that day.

By late February their cows had eaten all the available grass on the farm. The paddocks where they were grazing had almost become pure dirt. It was summer time and there was a drought on so they had to bring hay in to feed their cows. They started doing this every day. Whenever I was returning home from work driving down the road just outside my house, they would be coming towards me driving in one vehicle, with another man following behind them in a separate vehicle towing hay in a trailer. They seemed to only come on the property to feed their cows at the time that they knew I would be arriving home from work. Some days I would be home at 4.30pm and they would be there then. On the days that I came home at 6pm or later they would be driving down the road past me to feed their cows then. One day I came home early at 3.30pm and even then, they were just driving to the place to feed their cows at that time. They seemed to pass me at the same spot every time.

I wondered how they knew when I was coming home. I wondered if they were living in the house on the other farm. I doubted it, as the electricity supply was no longer connected and the septic tank was cracked apart and not useable. The plumbing was non-existent since the pipes had rusted out many years ago and never been repaired and the water supply to the house was permanently turned off. I wondered whether they had a person waiting outside my school where I worked, watching to see when I left in the afternoons. I was sure that they had some sort of scheme happening. My thoughts kept going back to the conversation between Allen and Wayne all those years ago. This was the conversation that they had when they were discussing the changes in the rental tenancy laws. When I thought back to this conversation I thought, How true. That is exactly what he is trying to do here. He is trying to annoy me off the place.

My feelings of paranoia were increasing every day but I steadfastly would not give in to them. I rang the police, making a complaint about them driving down the road when I was also driving on the road. The police said that it is a difficult situation being a public road; they could argue that they had no other choice than to drive down the road, considering their need to drive to the farms. The police said that they would have a talk with them but they were having difficulty catching them before they had left the property. Eventually they managed to apprehend them some kilometres away from the farm, where they were given a warning to stay away from me. After this their cows were fed and attended to by a local man who worked as a freelance farm caretaker.

On 26th February, late in the afternoon they spent about an hour and a half walking around the paddock, preventing me from going down to tend to my animals. I felt annoyed with them because they were stealthily exerting control over me. They were well aware that I checked on my animals as soon as I arrived home from work so they chose to be there at that exact time. As they were returning from the back of the farm, my horses were looking at them over the fence. They started chasing my horses with their car, yelling at them and sounding the car horn to frighten them. The horses all galloped back towards the house, snorting and panting when they arrived, clearly distressed. They knew that this would upset me. I could not do much about it, as it would seem a pathetic argument if I tried to say they were in breach of the intervention order and they might counter argue that the horses decided to gallop on their own.

One Sunday morning in early March I was woken by a knock on my door. It was a neighbour who told me one of my horses was out on the road badly injured. I rushed down the road and found it had one of its legs badly cut. The skin was peeled right back to the bone. I had to slowly walk it back to the house and get the vet. After it was treated I went to see how it had got out of its paddock onto the street. I walked around the fence and found that the horse must have tried to jump over the front fence and caught one leg on the top wire. The wire was broken and there was skin, blood and hair on the broken ends of the wire. As I was walking around trying to find what caused the horse to jump over the fence, I found part of a broken stock whip on the ground. I never use a stock whip but I knew someone who did when he was herding his cattle on his farms. I felt sure that the horse must have been chased by someone to make it jump the fence. It was a very quiet horse and it had lived in all its life on the farm. The horses that it lived with were all related and they had lived together for all their lives. It would be most unusual for such a horse to gallop full speed across an open paddock to jump the front fence on its own accord. I felt that it had been chased by someone brandishing a stock whip. Not only would the accident cause me anguish if the injuries were serious enough they would render the horse worthless so I would not be able to sell her if I was in urgent needs of funds to pay legal costs.

Shortly after this incident my son Luke, daughter-in-law Carmelina and granddaughter moved in to live with me. The house was now occupied twenty-four hours a day. Rarely was there a time when no one was at home. Shortly after they had moved in the sensor lights stopped coming on during the night and the Bilks became less visible around the place. Maybe it was just coincidental. I do not know. The interesting thing was that now when I rang the police to complain about them, the first thing that the police would ask was, "Are there any children there?" I would say, "Yes, my five- year old granddaughter is with me." The police would come out and investigate immediately.

34. I Get Pulled up by the Police

It was March and Allen had been gone for one year now. His car registration and insurance were due to be renewed. The notice was sent to the farm address. As I was using the car for farm activities, my lawyer advised me to pay the registration and insurance on it. The car was a utility and I drove to the Cranbourne shops to buy stock feed and farm equipment, things that were too large to fit into my sedan. I also drove it to my work one day a week to give it a longer drive, as it is better for the engine in the long term if it has the occasional long trip. On this day, I was driving the Ute home after a particularly long and harrowing day at work. I was almost home when I noticed the blue flashing lights of a police vehicle in my rear view mirror. I wondered who they were after and was most surprised when they drove alongside my car and gestured for me to pull over to the side of the road. I hadn't been speeding. I hadn't broken any road rules and I didn't think that they wanted to test me for alcohol. So why was I being stopped?

The police officer approached me in the car and spoke to me very severely. "Is this your car, madam?" He asked. "No officer it belonged to my late partner." I replied without question.: "Why are you driving it?" He questioned. "He left it to me in his Will and I am entitled to drive it." I didn't like where this was going. "Show me your driver's licence. "He asked gruffly. I took my licence out of my purse and handed it to him. "Here it is." The officer looked at my licence. "Is this your current address?" "Yes, officer." I replied. "This is not the last registered address for this vehicle." I was getting worried about whether Beryl had changed the car's registration into her own name. Me: "My street number is 200 but my partner had two properties on the same street and the registration address for this vehicle is for the property further down the street, number 250." "Madam, this vehicle is unregistered!" "What! I paid the registration two weeks ago. "I protested. "I repeat madam; this vehicle IS UNREGISTERED. You cannot drive this vehicle on the road. I don't know that you have the right to be in possession of this vehicle. What proof do you have to show me that you haven't stolen it?" At this point I burst into tears. I was tired, I was not thinking rationally, this man was speaking harshly to me, and I could not understand what was going on. I hadn't done anything wrong. The car was registered; I had paid it myself. I reached into the glove box and got out the registration paper with the receipt for payment attached to it. I gave it to him.

It was obvious that the registration had been paid two weeks earlier. I told him about the problems that I was having with the Bilks and the things that they were doing to me. The officer looked perplexed and told me to wait for a minute and he went to his car and got in. He returned with a much more sympathetic demeanour and told me that he had been in contact with the Cranbourne Police station and they corroborated my story about the harassment that I was being subjected to. They had a lengthy record on file, including information on the Intervention Orders. He had also been in contact with the vehicle registration office and they informed him that the car had in fact been re-registered but the registration had been cancelled two days previously. I was not allowed to drive the car home and had to get a tow truck to transport it home for me. The officer kindly helped me and drove me home. He gave me his contact details and told me that I could telephone him if I needed any urgent help and he would try to make sure that someone would assist me.

The next day I contacted the vehicle registration office and found out that the executor of the estate had cancelled the car's registration and had the money that I paid transferred into the estate bank account. I also contacted the car insurance company and found out a similar story. All my money was now in the estate coffers and I could not get it back. In addition, I had to pay for the truck that transported the car to my home. In all, I was close to a thousand dollars out of pocket. If I wanted to re-register the car I had to take it to a mechanic to get it checked for its roadworthiness, which would cost me even more money. There was no guarantee that Beryl wouldn't cancel the registration on me again if I did register it. I had my own car to drive so I decided that it wasn't worth having two registered vehicles. I put the expense down as a bad experience. I only drove the Ute on the farm from then on.

35. The Undertaking Agreement to Leave Me Alone!!!

Because Beryl and Wayne did not attend the January 17th intervention order hearing it was rescheduled for April 4th. As the date loomed my lawyers suggested that the two parties sign an Undertaking to leave each other alone, as this would be a lot cheaper than fighting the order in court. This seemed a good idea to me, as each court date cost about $4,000 for legal representation. If the other party chose to drag the case out it could end up costing me a lot more. Cost was not a problem for them, as they were using the estate money. Wayne boasted to people that he didn't care whether it cost all of the money in the estate; he would make sure that I never got the farm. Their lawyer declared to my lawyer that they would fight the case until they won. I didn't have a chance. The day before the court date the agreement was signed. It was more beneficial for them to sign it than for me, as they would have ended up with criminal records if they had lost.

They never turned up at the court and their lawyer appeared on their behalf. He stated to my lawyer that they could not come as it was too distressing for them. They were the ones persecuting me and they said that they were distressed! It was their choice to do this! I was willing to settle on the February 2006 Will but they were not. Although they had all reached an agreement and signed the Undertaking documentation, the lawyers and I still had to attend the court at their appointed time and speak before the judge. Neville McNaughton was there as the lawyer representing them, and I was there with Oona Macafferty, my lawyer. The three of us sat together in the court and chatted with each other while waiting for the judge. Their lawyer seemed like quite a nice man, not the slightest bit evil as I had expected. Judging by their lawyer's reaction when he was introduced to me, I got the distinct impression that he was expecting a woman of a very different appearance. Within days of the April 4th hearing the Bilks changed law firms again. Gordon Richly was their new man, taking over the case.

Throughout the months of persecution that I was being subjected to, I was becoming so distressed that I was regularly getting into a state of panic. It was at these times that I would ring up my lawyer, and he was always very calming and reassuring. I would be so distressed I would speak to him way too rapidly. Thomas would say to me, "Slow down, slow down, my brain cannot process information at that speed." I would have to take a breath and try to calm down. Talking to him would always help me to de-stress. He would answer my questions and state precisely what my options were. He would tell me that my case was like peeling an onion: "You have to start at the outer layer and peel off one layer at a time. You will eventually get to the centre." He knew what he was talking about and he made me feel that I was being looked after. I always ended up feeling calm and relieved after I had spoken with him as he was always steady, honest and dependable. I was very pleased that I had him on my side.

A few weeks later the latest lawyer, Gordon Richly, wrote to mine, requesting my permission for them to use the cattle stockyards so they could truck their cows off the farm. The stockyards were located about fifty metres from my house so they could not use them without being in breach of the Undertaking agreement. I gave permission through my lawyers and stayed inside on the designated day and time. They did not show up but I heard cows mooing and people yelling out on the road. They ended up taking their cows away by herding them out through the side gate and walking them down the road to the other farm. I had farm peace at last! Maybe!

36. The Harassment Continues in a Different Form; Strange Telephone Calls

The cows leaving the farm did not mean total peace for me. It was at about this time that the strange telephone calls started. It is normal for people to receive telemarketing phone calls, particularly in the evenings. I often got my share even though I was on the 'Do Not Call' register but in addition I received other calls that seemed out of the ordinary. There were the calls that had no person on the other end of the line. They seemed to be made from a public place such as a hotel or restaurant. I could easily comprehend conversations in the background but no one spoke on the phone. In one conversation, it sounded like there was a group of women talking about their boyfriends. In another one there seemed to be men talking about football and sports. I was able to hear what was being said but no one could hear me calling out, "Hello! Is anyone there?" I often left the phone on the kitchen bench for an hour or two, and when I returned the phone was still online but the voices seemed to be different, with different conversations happening. I felt that the calls were being made from public telephones and the phone receiver was left sitting off the hook. I contacted the telephone company to put a trace on. When the next call happened, I had to dial a certain number to get the caller identified. I found that phone call was made from a public bar in a Melbourne city hotel. It was not possible to identify who the caller was. Soon after I had put the call tracing in place these odd calls stopped happening.

Other unusual calls were made from official places, or so it seemed. While my mother was staying with me she usually answered the telephone and took messages. One call was from the Australian Bureau of Statistics wanting information about the cattle on the farm. Every year farmers are sent a Census form to fill in giving details of the farming activities carried out on their farm during the previous year. The Census Bureau wanted information such as the type and number of animals that were kept on the farm, whether the farmer grew crops and the area of land that was used for cropping and various similar farm related specific information. Allen hated filling in the Census form, as he felt that it was 'Big Brother' watching over him. While she was alive May filled in the Census form every year, and after she died Allen passed the task on to me. In the year 2001, he decided that he did not want to fill in the Census form anymore. He did not want me to do it for him; he simply wanted to be removed from the Census database.

He dictated a letter for me to write in the 'Further Information' space on the form: 'Elderly owner in poor state of health. Property has been destocked for many months and no figures are available. The property is up for sale.' I complied with his wishes and filled it in as he instructed me, and he signed it. I posted the form off, and that was the last I heard from the Bureau of Statistics until 2008. The caller identified herself as a person who worked for the Bureau and asked to speak to me by name. My mother told her that I was not available at the moment and said, "Could you leave a message?" The caller stated that she was making a follow-up call about the 2001 farm census. She wanted some further information and she recited the information that I had written on the form for Allen. The caller stated that the form was filled in by me, as it was in my handwriting, and signed by him. She would not leave a contact number and asked when would be a good time to ring to get me. My mother gave her some suggested times for her to ring but she never called back.

The Census forms were sent to the farmers in duplicate so the farmer could fill both forms in at the same time. One form was to be sent to the Bureau and the other was to be kept by the farmer. I checked the copy that I had and there was no way the caller or anyone in the Bureau of Statistics could know my name or whose handwriting was on the form. A lot of government forms had a section where the person who filled in the information wrote their name and details, but on this form there was no such section. There was absolutely no identifying information for the Bureau to know who wrote on the form. I made a follow-up call to the Bureau but they could not help me. I was not able to find out who called me from the Bureau--or if anyone actually did, which I doubted. I wondered whether the Bilks wanted to check how many cows that Allen had written on the form as being owned by him. They did not have any access to his financial records, so they had no legal proof about the stock on the property. They did not want to acknowledge that I owned any of the farm livestock or that I had a right to ownership of all the stock due to Allen and my joint ownership. Any jointly owned assets become the property of the surviving partner. In this case all livestock were owned jointly, so they were now legally mine.

Another call that was answered by my mother was from the Teacher's Union. The caller had a telephone survey that she wanted to me to answer. She did not leave a return number either but stated that she would call another time. I was not a member of the 'Teacher's Union' and felt that the call was very odd. I was a member of the Australian Education Union. I called the office and a representative assured me that no one from that union would have made a call requesting answers to a survey. Any survey would have been sent by a letter in the mail.

Two government departments audited me. The first was the Livestock Production Assurance section of the Cattle Council of Australia and the other was from the Taxation Department. Government departments randomly audit people from time to time. These were genuine audits but it seemed peculiar to me that two government departments would choose to audit me at around the same time. It could have been simply coincidental and I was being paranoid. Fortunately for me, I had all my bookkeeping records and receipts up to date and the audits were no more than an inconvenience. Both auditors were friendly and helpful and I had a good chat with each of them. They passed on some useful information that I could use in the future. I passed both audits perfectly. When I told the people that I worked with about the surveys and audits there was not one other person who had been contacted by the union to answer a survey. No one knew anyone else who had been called either. No one from my work had ever been audited by the tax department. I felt certain that I had been set-up by someone. My boss said, "You must be as pure as the snow. If your ex-step-relatives could get something on you they would have surely done it by now."

37. Some Unusual People Become Part of My Life

Car Man

I am not sure exactly when the 'car man', as I decided to call him, first appeared. A man started parking and sitting in his old car along the farm's side road near the same gate that the Bilks used when they wanted to harass me with their cows. The car was about one hundred metres from my home but I could see it in the distance through my bedroom window. The farmhouse was mostly surrounded by trees but the car was parked so that it was visible to my house through a small gap in the trees. The position of the car also gave it a clear view of my front gate so that anyone entering or leaving the property could be observed. Whenever I drove through my front gate I could see it. I felt sure that I was under surveillance but I could not prove it. The man would sit in the car for about eight to ten hours every day.

I experienced my first encounter with him one dark night as I returned home from work. I had had some problems with hoon drivers on that road. It was a gravel road and they enjoyed doing burnouts and wheelies along the road. On occasions, they would lose control of their cars and smash through my fence. I had to keep checking the side fence every day so that I could fix any breaks before any of my animals escaped. On my way home from work I would make a quick detour down the side road and back to check on the fence. I saw him there in his car but I did not give him much thought, initially. After he had been sitting there for a few weeks my son called the police and made a complaint about him being there. The next day when I arrived home and made my usual drive down the road he was standing in the middle of the road blocking my way. He was a large man, thickset, at least 180cm tall. He was wearing dirty tracksuit pants with a windcheater, unshaven and had long greasy hair, what was left of it that is. He was partially bald. His presence was very intimidating but he was standing in the centre of the road. It is a narrow dead end street so I could not turn around and go any other way. I had to stop but I locked all my doors and kept my window wound up. He abused me because someone had rung the police about him being there. After he approached my side of my car I managed to quickly drive around him and go home.

I was so shaken up by the experience that my foot shook uncontrollably on the accelerator pedal. I could hardly keep it steady on the pedal. How dare he accost me like that! When I told my son after I arrived home and he immediately called the police. They came and saw us after they had spoken with Car Man and he had told them that it was a lovely, peaceful place to sit and listen to the football on the radio. This was on a Tuesday night and there was no football on the radio on a Tuesday as far as I knew.

It was winter when he started his parking habits, and it was getting dark earlier. I often arrived home from work after dark. I drove down the side road with my lights on high beam so that I could see the fence better. At the end of the road I would turn my car around and drive back to my house. On the second occasion that I drove down the road with my lights on, he was standing in the middle of the road again. I managed to drive around him. As I passed he abused me for driving along the road with my high beam lights on.

The police were called again and they spoke to him again. They came to my house and told me that there was nothing that they could do to make him move. It was a public road and he was quite entitled to park there. My son had a talk with him but that did not resolve anything. He said that he was living with his mother and he needed to get out of the house. He liked parking there and he didn't intend to move. A few days later I was talking with a neighbour about the high beam light incident. I did not tell him to do anything to Car Man but he decided on his own undertaking to annoy him.

He went parking behind his car, shining his high beam lights on him. When I arrived home that night car man was not in his usual position and as I neared my driveway to my house I found my wheelie bins in the middle of my gateway, forcing me to get out and move them before I could drive through. I did not want to get out of my car in the dark in case he was hiding in the trees and bushes around the gate. I felt positive that someone was lurking nearby, in the shadows and the bins were a trap for me to force me out of my car but I couldn't see anything. I suspected that it could have been him who did this because it was something unusual that had never happened to me before and he was a recent arrival who had harassed me already. Luke wasn't home and I was too afraid to get out of my car so I rang my neighbour to get him to come and help me and he told me what he had done. I asked him not to do it again in case of possible repercussions.

With all the hours that he spent sitting in his car, I puzzled over what he was doing for a toilet. I often wondered whether I would stumble over a pile of human excrement while walking around my paddock. He alternated between coming early in the mornings and staying parked for about ten hours before leaving again and coming later in the day and staying there until late in the night. If he was parked there when I went to bed at night I sensed him out there there… Staring….. Watching. Even though I had the window blinds down I could sense him there. It gave me chills. Sometimes I woke up in the night imagining him peering through the space between the edge of the blind and the window. I imagined that I could see his eye reflected in the mirror that I had by the edge of the window. In my dreams, I saw his eye peering at me. One night I could not bear it anymore. I knew that it was impossible for him to be there without setting the sensor lights on but I moved the mirror anyway. He always parked in the exact same spot. Any farther north or south would place him out of view from my house or front gateway due to the trees. I tried putting logs of wood at that spot when he wasn't around so he had to park somewhere else but he moved the wood and parked exactly in that spot. I felt that I was under surveillance but I could not prove it. An interesting thing about life is the way people adjust to situations, whether they are good or bad. Initially Car Man caused me to feel stressed and apprehensive about his presence.

After a while his car became a fixture that one checked for as one drove by. Ah! Car Man is there! Eventually his presence was not noticed. It was when his car was not there that I became stressed again. Where is he? Is he parked somewhere else? Has he gone? Will he come back? Will someone else come in his place? All these thoughts would play in my mind. I did not like the idea that I could see him parked there from my house and he could see my house, so I came up with a plan to block his view. Many years earlier there was a high wooden paling fence on that side of the house. It provided a wind break for the house when there were no trees around it. The fence fell into disrepair because many trees had been planted and they had grown large enough to provide both shade and a wind break. The posts were still in the ground so I only had to nail new timber rails and wooden palings onto them. I bought new timber rails and palings. One weekend Luke and I set to work and rebuilt the fence. We made it a little higher than the earlier fence had been so the house was hidden behind it. We also transplanted some large hedge plants that were near the other side of the house down the driveway to hide it from the side road. A few days later Car Man disappeared. Just as suddenly as he had appeared, he was suddenly gone. We never saw him or his car again. Unfortunately for other people, Car Man and the fence- smashing hoons had left me and my family feeling extremely jumpy about people stopping along that road. There are no houses on that section of road so whenever we saw someone parked there we immediately wondered why.

About a week after his disappearance, I was walking in the paddock outside the renewed paling fence when I saw another car parked in the same place where he had used to park. A man was out of his car and a look at him through binoculars revealed that he had a camera on a tripod. My daughter–in-law Carmelina was home with me, and I went inside the house and told her. Where I hid and looked through binoculars wondering what to do, Carmelina was the opposite to me, she was fearless and confronted people. She had just had a shower and was only wearing a towel. She quickly pulled on some tracksuit trousers and a top and ran to her car, shoeless, braless and panty less. She zoomed down the drive and then sped up the road to where the man was standing. She was driving way too fast and when she slammed on the brakes near the man's car, her car slid in the gravel along the road to a halt. The rear end of her car fishtailed, nearly causing her car to spin. Thankfully she is a very good driver and she never lost control of her car. "WHAT THE HELL ARE YOU DOING?" she yelled at him (the spoken expletives have been omitted for politeness). The man visibly cringed; he looked like he could have had an underwear accident. "I'm just taking some pictures of the sunset," he stammered back. "Here, look at the pictures." She realised that he was genuine and apologised to him and told him that we had been having trouble with some people breaking our fences and gates and we were becoming very suspicious of strangers. The man packed up his things and left straight afterwards. He must have decided that it was not such a nice place to take pictures, after all.

Spy Guy

At about the same time that Car Man was parking by the farm, a new teacher was employed on a short-term contract at my work. I decided to call him 'Spy Guy.' He was one of four short term contract teachers that were employed at that time but this man stood out because he seemed to hone in on me in an unusual way. Teachers seem to spend a good proportion of their after-school hours in meetings. At the conclusion of one of the afternoon meetings everyone left the room except for him and me. He started up a conversation with me and said, "You look like a clever woman. I am paying too much tax. Do you have any ideas how I can avoid paying tax?" I laughed at him and said, "Not a clue. I pay my tax and that is that." He persisted, "But you must know of some schemes that you use." I was rather disinterested in his conversation at this point, but felt it had deeper undertones. You don't start asking tax questions when you first meet someone. "I don't have any schemes. Go and see an accountant. I am not an accountant." I replied, hoping the conversation would change and my paranoia about everyone new I meet would be dispelled. "Do you know a good accountant who could help me?" he asked. I almost wondered for a moment what trouble he was in himself, then my wariness kicked in again. I was not volunteering my Accountant! "I'm sorry, I can't help you," I said ending the conversation completely and walking away. I busied myself with something that didn't involve him. The next week after the staff meeting he decided to chat with me again. This time about travel and which countries we would like to visit, what things we would like to see when he started another line of strange questions. He asked me, "Do you pick up men to have sex with them when you are overseas?" "Of course not!" I replied. "I am way too disease-phobic for that." He persisted, in an unusual way, I had not discussed my partner with him or my circumstances. We were not friends this new teacher and me. He seemed to know a lot about me. I assumed I was not the source of gossip amongst teachers at the school and why would any of them volunteer such in-depth information to him unless he had been fishing for it. "What about when your partner was alive; did you have lots of lovers?" "No!" This is not an appropriate conversation for a workplace." Let's change the topic," I told him indignantly. I was very shocked by the things that he was saying to me. My school was staffed by quite staid people and he was undeniably crossing the boundaries of politeness and political correctness. I had never had anyone ask me such questions about my overseas trips before. I never would have thought to ask such questions of anyone else.

Schools have libraries of computer programs and DVD movies. As part of my job I had to keep track of the originals and lend them out to people whenever they wanted to borrow them. I was very efficient and the school never lost any original DVDs while I was overseeing them. Spy Guy wanted me to make pirate copies of certain DVD movies and computer programmes so he could use them at home. I would tell him the same thing that I told other people at my work. "I don't have any pirate copies of movies. I buy originals and so should you. If you want copies you will have to make them yourself."

Over the next few weeks he would quiz me, trying to get information out of me. He wanted to know whether I had any ideas on how he could make more money, cash in hand, without declaring the income on his tax. He had this brilliant idea that he wanted to start his own school. He needed funding and he quizzed me about whether I had any money and if I would be interested in becoming a silent partner in his school venture. He asked me, "I need about fifty thousand dollars to get started. Would you have fifty thousand dollars to invest?" Or maybe even sixty thousand?" I told him of ways that he could apply for government small business grants to get funding to start up a new business and he could get a grant of fifty thousand dollars. He did not seem to be interested in my suggested ways to access funding and it seemed to me he was trying to find out how much available money I had.

I was becoming so paranoid that my work colleagues were questioning my sanity. I recalled an evening Current Affairs Story that was featured on TV some weeks before Spy Guy first came to work at my school. The story featured a Private Investigator company and it gave information on the services that were provided by the company. Among the services offered was employee investigation for companies. If a company suspected an employee of theft or fraud they could engage the services of an investigator to work within the company and glean the required information.

I rang up some private investigator companies trying to find out whether a person could be employed to become an employee in a school to get information. Most were very wary about giving out too much information. I had one man admit that he had done this and employed people with the appropriate qualifications to fill an available vacancy when one came up to investigate an individual or people or a company. He told me that it cost a lot of money to employ someone for such a job. Obviously, this would not be a problem for the Bilks! He mentioned that he personally did a surveillance job like that and he had to drive an old car instead of his nice BMW, dress in old clothes and work at a job in a factory where he had no idea what he was doing. He felt that he appeared stupid in that instance and he did not particularly like doing it. He did not tell me whether it was a successful operation or not. Spy Guy drove a Datsun Bluebird and was always crying poor and wearing tattered, frayed, holey clothes. What's more, he had only just moved into the flat where he lived a couple of weeks before he got the job at my work. I wondered whether he had been paid to apply for the position so that he could fish for information about me.

My case was costing a lot of money, which I was funding on my own. The Bilks were using the estate money to fund their side. If they thought that I did not have enough money to keep going with my side of the case, they would have an advantage over me. I pointed out to

Spy Guy that I had a very comfortable income with my wages, farming income and business investments. I did not wish to take on any other business such as his school idea. Some people might think that he was looking for a woman with wealth, but he did not seem interested in me as someone that he wanted to have a relationship with nor was he my type. I was not looking for a relationship anyway. Always in the back of my mind I thought about one of my neighbour's comments that he regularly made to me: "If your case goes to court the one with the most money always wins. They will win because they have more money than you. They will be able to keep the case going until you run out of money." Beryl and Wayne needed to know how much financial backing I would have if they went to court. They needed to break me financially so that I would give up the case.

Spy Guy started trying to get himself an invite to my place. "Do you have a horse that I could ride?" he asked. "Do you have any blackberries that I could come and pick? What about mushrooms; are there any wild mushrooms in your paddocks? Wild mushrooms taste the best; they have a lot more favour that the ones that you buy in the shops." I was curious as to why he wanted to see where I lived and I wondered if I could find out anything more about him so I told him he could come to my place to pick mushrooms, as they were in season now. He came out the next Saturday and I had to admit it was a fun day. He made me laugh with his unique sense of humour. We ran around searching for suitable mushrooms and he would make comments on the quality of the mushrooms. Whenever we found a sickly one he would comment, "This one is no good; it's got 'The AIDS'." Despite the mushroom picking activity, I felt that a lot of the conversation was steered towards him trying to get information. I was becoming very suspicious of him and I thought of the tax audit that had already been done. I also thought back to my first visit to a lawyer some years before, where I was asked what things I knew about Allen that I could use against him. The lawyer asked me whether he had any tax issues and whether he used any tax avoidance schemes. Allen never used any tax reduction schemes; he paid the tax that he was due to pay and accepted it. I wondered whether Spy Guy was trying to find out things from me that could be used against me in a court case.

One day I just came right out and confronted him. "Why do you keep asking me these things? Are you being paid to spy on me or something? Are you trying to get information out of me? I don't do anything illegal; what do you want from me?" He didn't answer me. I decided if he was really being paid to spy on me, I would give him false information. I started making up stories to tell him. If he wasn't spying on me, too bad! If he was, then it would be interesting to see the outcome. I asked other colleagues whether he had asked them for ideas on how to cheat the tax system and they told me no. It was suggested that he must have thought I was very smart and might have some good ideas. Ideas on how to be a crook! Sure, how did he come to that conclusion? He didn't know me!

I discovered that Beryl and Wayne seemed to know details about my employment, such as my teaching pay level and the other allowances that I received for extra duties that I carried out in my position. I wondered how they could have found out this information. I never discussed details about my employment with my friends or neighbours. They were things that they would have to have learnt by talking to people with whom I worked. They had inside information on me about things that had happened at my work after Allen had died, so they were things that they could not have found out from him.

Soon after my confrontation with him, Spy Guy broke his contract and left the school. He did this two weeks before the school holidays were due to start, and he missed out on the holiday pay. No one breaks their contract before the holidays because they don't want to miss out on the free pay. His leaving suddenly created a problem because he didn't give notice. He just left and he had to be replaced immediately for the final two weeks of the term. This is only a short summary of some of his interactions with me, taken from my diary notes. I suppose I was becoming too paranoid but I was convinced that he was only working there to spy on me. It was not so much the fact that he was asking me such unusual questions but the way he asked me things. He never did it in front of anyone else, only when we were alone in our staff workroom and he often behaved as if he was hiding something. He lived in North Melbourne, an area where a lot of our work colleagues also lived. If any of our colleagues accidentally came across him in the city, when they tried to get his attention he would glance in their direction but act like he didn't see them and run away. They all thought that his behaviour at the time as weird.

38. The End is in Sight--Maybe!

Probate was eventually applied for on January 30th, 2009. The Will case could finally progress! The proceeding was commenced at the end of February 2009. A check on the Supreme Court of Victoria Probate Office web page listed the Probate application as being refused. They were locked into continuing with the case, as they could not do anything more with the estate beyond what they were already getting away with.

At the next directions hearing on March 29th a timeline was set for each of the parties to file their affidavits and evidence. Affidavits are written documents prepared by each party and their witnesses outlining the information that they are going to use in their defence when the case goes to court.

1. Within 14 days I had to submit reasons for my objection to the probate being granted on the 2007 Will.

2. Beryl had to file and serve any affidavits upon which she intended to rely upon by 13 July 2009.

3. I had to file and serve any affidavits by 13 October 2009.

4. Beryl had to file and serve any further affidavits in reply by 13 November 2009.

5. A mediation had to be completed by 13 December 2009.

6. Both parties had 60 days to make discovery of all medical reports, records, testamentary scripts and writings etc.

Make discovery meant that both sides had to find everything official that existed that they wanted to use to defend their side of the court case. There were a few other 'housekeeping' orders to be complied with as well. I filed my reasons for my objection to probate being granted by the due date. July came and went. Nothing happened with their defence. Beryl ignored the orders. Between August and December, we received no communication whatsoever.

It was Christmas again! Everything stopped until the New Year. Dates for directions hearings in the courts were set and had to be postponed due to the inactivity of the Bilks. Early in 2010 at another directions hearing, another set of dates for affidavits to be served, etc. were made:

- They had to issue any subpoenas for medical files by March.
- 17 March Beryl's affidavit had to be filed.
- 31 May my response had to be filed.
- 30 June all final affidavit material had to be filed.
- The final order was that mediation was to occur by 31 July.

Again, all orders were ignored along with all lawyer threats and court orders. The litigants could apply to the listing Master for an extension of time if they could not comply with the orders and submit the required documents by the due dates. Beryl did not bother with applying for any extension of time; she simply ignored all orders. At the next directions hearing the Judge told off their lawyer, Gordon Richley, because his clients had not made any attempt to obtain the required records and had not submitted their evidence by the due dates. That was the full extent of the punishment meted out by the court system. When it comes to the law, if people choose to thumb their nose at it then they can get away with anything, it seems.

Throughout this intervening time period my lawyer was working hard at obtaining Allen's nursing home files and various other documents that we needed to support our case. It was a difficult task. No one wanted to risk being embroiled in their own litigation from other parties because files were given to me that I did not have a right to access. Signed requests were usually required from both parties to the litigation, and Beryl ignored any demand to countersign with me. The case was stagnating because my side could not access any files and without affidavits I did not know how she intended to make her case.

I decided that some R & R was needed, so it was off to Ireland for a glorious four-week jaunt.

The unsworn affidavits made by Beryl, Wayne, Neville McNaughton, and the two Will signing witnesses, Ralph and Steven Daunton, were finally sent on 15 August 2010. There was very little information contained in them. Thomas estimated in the time it took for them to be written, the other side must have written at the rate of one word a day. "That is the way that Wayne operates," I explained to him. "Do not give too much away; see what the other side has first." I suggested to him that they probably wanted to find out what evidence I had before they wrote any lengthy affidavits. They didn't want to give away any unnecessary information. In the past Wayne had told Allen that he always relied on his opponents missing out on something that could be vital, leading to a situation which he could use to his own advantage. Unsworn affidavits are not legally enforceable, as the people making them have not signed to claim that they are true. They can change them if they learn something new. I wrote my responses to their affidavits but nothing was sent on to their lawyer because my side was waiting for the official sworn affidavits to be submitted first.

About a month later sworn affidavits from the same people were submitted. There were a few changes made between the sworn and the unsworn affidavits. The main changes made were to any references made about me that could have led the reader to imply there was a relationship between Allen and me. These were removed. Any mention of me had me noted as 'a friend'.

I sent my affidavit responses and waited for further responses from the other party. Wait, wait, wait! Then wait a little more!

We managed to obtain Allen's nursing home files without Beryl's compliance by exploring another avenue of law. It took quite a few months of negotiation between the lawyers for the nursing home and mine.

It was time to try for a mediation date but that was difficult to arrange because Christmas was here again! The case would sit in abeyance until the New Year.

39. More Intimidation: The Drive-bys

Beryl and Wayne seemed to have been affected by the submission of the affidavits. They tried a new intimidation tactic. For the months from the end of 2009 through early 2010 they started the 'Drive-Bys'. The 'Drive- Bys seemed to happen every week and sometimes a couple of times a week. I loved my evening walk to the back of the farm and home again. I looked at the cows, patted the friendlier ones and then spent time with my horses. I knew all the cows, but some were more special. There was Garden Cow, the one I regularly let into the garden to mow the lawn around my house. Usually if cows are put into a new place they stress out and produce vast quantities of watery, squirty manure rather than soft lumps that can be easily shovelled away. Garden Cow was always relaxed while in the garden. She would eat her fill and wait at the gate to be let out again. I had had her since she was about nine months old. When I bought her it was a drought year and I had plenty of grass in the paddock; however, Garden Cow had arrived with a habit of putting her head through the fence to eat the grass on the other side. She was growing horns and every day she would get her horns stuck in the fence. I had to help her get her horns untangled. She became very friendly from receiving this daily handling.

There was Smithers, the cow that was born as the result of one of our neighbour's (the Smithers) bulls jumping the fence and jumping her mother. Smithers's first calf was stillborn. When I walked down the paddock on the day that she had calved, I could see that she had recently had a calf but I couldn't see it anywhere. Smithers led me over to the bushes where her dead calf lay. She kept looking back and forth between me and her calf as if to say, "Make it get up like the other calves." I had to tell her that it would not get up, ever.

Another pet cow was Panda Eyes (a self-explanatory name). She was born on the farm. One day I saw that she was limping quite badly. I got her into the cow yards and discovered that she had a coiled car spring from an old wrecked car on the farm wrapped around her leg. The leg was black and so was the spring, so it was not easy to see. She must have got it over her foot when she was small and her leg grew until the spring was cutting into her skin. Luke and I had to cut the spring off with an angle grinder, as it was made from too strong a metal for bolt cutters. I had to keep pouring cold water on the spring and leg while Luke cut the metal. In spite of the water the spring kept heating up and it must have hurt a bit, as Panda remembers the treatment and shakes her head at me whenever I go by her. I think she is trying to tell me that her leg is fine now and she doesn't need any more treatment.

It is not a good idea to make good friends of the cows; they end up dying of old age on the farm because friends can't be eaten. Despite this, the cows would get their evening petting. Before venturing out I had to kit myself out with my mobile phone, binoculars and camera. The phone was to call for help if I had a problem. The camera was to photograph anything that may have been damaged like gates or fences or suspicious looking marks like car tyre marks on the ground indicating someone had been on the property. The binoculars were for me to check for suspicious things in the distance before walking toward anything like that. I had become dependent on my safety kit and could not go for a walk without it.

In addition to my safety kit I always felt that I had divine help in the form of Allen's spirit watching over me while I was walking. Or maybe I was just psychic! Often as I was walking along paying attention to my cows I would suddenly get a premonition to look over towards the road. Every time I had one of these premonitions Wayne and Beryl would be there driving along the road slowly or standing at the fence looking at me. I never got one of these premonitions when they weren't there. I would thank Allen for the warning because I was sure he was watching over me. I often stood still, watching them. They would drive slowly up the road, turn around and drive back down the road, then back again. They would do this three or four times, sometimes taking ten or fifteen minutes at the task. Usually they would get out of their car and look at me over the fence.

I would look at them through my binoculars, looking back at me through their binoculars. They always maintained a two hundred metre separation distance so that I would not have grounds to reinstate my Intervention Order. It was something that could be done at any time, according to the court orders. They often drove different cars to try to fool me but when they got out of the car I knew it was them. I could tell by the way they walked, even if I couldn't easily discern their features. All people have their own distinctive walking pattern, and I usually recognize people by their walking style first. Also, I have such excellent long distance vision that I can see distant objects far better than many people more than half my age, including my teenaged school students.

In 2010 the case was continuing. Beryl's lawyers informed my lawyer that she had to go away for her work, leading to a six-week delay. Next Wayne had to go away--another three-week delay. After that, their lawyer was taking long service leave, leading to another three months' delay! Then their barrister went on leave, another four weeks' delay. I decided that I was not going to let them dictate my life and ruin it. I would also take advantage of the lull in the case. New York, followed by two weeks in San Francisco, was the stress relief for me this time. A mediation date was set for October 21st, 2010.

40. Another Mediation

The mediation happened on the scheduled date. I was extremely apprehensive about this mediation because unlike the previous two mediations, all parties were going to be sitting in the same room. This time Luke accompanied me, along with my lawyer and a barrister. When we arrived at the venue for the mediation we met the representatives for the opposing party, namely Gordon Richley, with his barrister. Beryl and Wayne were not present and we presumed that they were already in the meeting room. We were all introduced to each other, and I was amazed at Gordon Richley's response when he met me. He looked me up and down, then he seemed to turn a little pale at first and then his face went red. While everyone was talking small talk, he stared at me and looked very disturbed. I felt certain that I did not look like he expected me to look. He then said, "Excuse me. I know that this is highly irregular and I have never done something like this before, but I need some time to talk with my clients before we begin the mediation." He then disappeared with his barrister into the room that I presumed was to be the place for the mediation. My entourage and I were left standing, twiddling our thumbs and wondering what was going on. My lawyer and barrister were speculating as to whether the mediation was likely to be going ahead. They both said that this had never happened to them before at a mediation meeting.

We were left standing and waiting for about half an hour. Gordon Richley returned and apologized for delaying us. He informed us that his clients would still like to have the mediation. We all entered the room but I knew from the outset that the meeting would not end up with any result. Confidentiality regulations prevent me from writing about what was discussed in that meeting. When I entered the room, I felt like I was under a microscope. I was pleased that I had spent time preparing myself.

Both the barrister and lawyer for the Bilks stared at me for most of the time that they were in the room. I got the feeling that they expected me to have horns growing from my head. I wondered what sort of assessment they were making of me. I felt that I probably did not look the way they had presupposed I would look. They may have been thinking that they would have trouble convincing a judge that no relationship had existed between Allen and me. The part about Allen feeling embarrassed about my relationship claims, as his daughter had declared, might be difficult to prove.

I felt that I had presented myself very well. I had carefully chosen my ensemble to make me look the worthy partner that I was. My hair had been styled that morning and I also had my makeup professionally applied. I was grateful for the genes that I had inherited from my grandmother that gave me such good skin tone in my more mature years. I had planned it well and I looked absolutely fabulous on that day. Needless to say, Beryl and Wayne both looked quite haggard and drawn. Trying to pull off a lie was taking its toll on their appearance. Wayne looked like he hated me, which I felt sure was true. I thought that I could see steam rising from his reddened face. As I expected, no settlement occurred at that mediation. Within days of the mediation my lawyers were informed that they had changed lawyers again! They engaged another legal firm, headed by Tiffany Washingham of Washingham and Partners.

The new lawyers needed time to review the case! A request for an extension of time was made. Oh! Gosh! Christmas was here again! Nothing would happen until the New Year!

41. A Time to Spy

It was late 2010 and the case was going nowhere fast. It had been nearly four years since Allen died and there had been nothing but inactivity and delay. I decided that my only course of action was to see whether I could find a person associated with the Bilks who had similar handwriting to the signature on the Will. I presumed that there was a possibility that they could have used someone to impersonate Allen and sign the Will on 25 February 2007.

I needed to figure out who the man was that they could have used. I decided that the person would need to be someone whom they had known for many years who could be trusted by them and had to be old to pass for Allen. I knew all the relatives on Beryl's side and figured that she did not have any male relatives who could pass as her father. I tried to remember all the likely people in Wayne's life that I had heard Allen mention. He had a farm north of Melbourne, and Allen had told me about a few old men that lived in that area who had helped Wayne on his farm. The problem was finding the person's name. I knew some by their nicknames and another who lived in a shipping container on his farm. Shipping Container man, as I referred to him, had had a very long association with them. I had to come up with an idea. I was too frightened of Wayne to go to the town where his farm was situated and ask people. It would be just my luck to be in the area when he turned up. He would probably love the idea of taking out an intervention order against me. Worse still, his car was a large four-wheel drive and I had a sedan. He could easily run into my car and nudge it over a steep edge of the road on an isolated hilly stretch. I'd observed his anger when he was at my place. I was not sure how much he would lose control if he saw me. Going to the town was out of the question.

My first thought was to search through the electoral rolls. That meant a trip into Melbourne City to the State Library. The town where the farm was located had a small population; only a couple of hundred people lived in the area. It should not be too difficult. I started my search on the next weekend. Once I started I realized that it was going to be a time consuming activity. Wayne had threatened to drag the case out for ten years and it had only been four years so far. There was another six years to go, so I knew that I would have a lot of time to do it. I at least felt that I was doing something rather than sitting and waiting, afraid of what would be likely to be done to me next. I had a focus, even if it was an unusual focus. I spent Saturday scanning microfiche sheets that listed the names and addresses of registered voters for the area in 2007. That was the year that Allen died. I ran out of time and had a headache so on Sunday I took a camera with me and rapidly took photos of each screen without looking at the information. This way I could read the sections at home whenever I had a little free time. I wrote down the names of every enrolled male living in the area. That gave me the addresses of the men but I had no idea of their ages.

Plan two: check older rolls to see whether the men still lived in the area at an earlier year. My idea was to work backwards to a year when the person was not on the roll, the idea being before he turned eighteen and first enrolled or had moved into the area. This presented its own set of problems. Electoral boundaries are changed regularly, so the town was in one electorate in one year and another in another year. The search became easier as I searched through more ancient rolls because the names were listed alphabetically, regardless of where the person lived and what the electorate was. This took me quite a few weekends over a period of a couple of months. Simultaneously, I was searching the Internet for the names to see whether any came up in a search engine. This enabled me to scratch quite a few names off the list, as younger people tended to have Facebook pages and the like and I could eliminate quite a few due to youth.

Library searching is quite a popular activity and there were many regulars who tended to chat to each other. It became quite a social activity for me. I felt that I needed to check the death records to find out whether any of the men on my list had died since 2007. One of the other searchers suggested I try the Ryerson Index. Oh! Wow! The Ryerson Index lists all the death notices published in the major daily papers throughout Australia. I could eliminate more names due to them dying but being the wrong age. The Index gives only basic information such as name, date of death and the paper in which the notice was published. I checked the death notices in the papers to find out more about the men who had died. Okay-I had names; I had ages and I had dead men, but I didn't have any handwriting. I found that the older men all seemed to have served in the war. Wayne's father had served in the Second World War. I searched the Internet for his old regiment. There was a complete website devoted to that regiment. Wow! There were heaps of old men. It listed every member and gave details about each one. When a soldier died there would be a written obituary, along with details about the person's funeral and who attended. Wayne was listed as a family member and there was even a photo of him attending a get-together in late 2006. Could he have recruited a person from this meeting?

His father and some of his war associates went on a memorial trip to the place where they saw action during the Second World War. Wayne was with them on this trip, so he knew these men. I had names but no handwriting. Another suggestion that was put to me was that I should check the war service records of his father's soldier associates. That was easy; it could be done on the Internet. The war service records have every filed bit of information for every Australian soldier who served in the war. Scanned copies of the original enlistment forms were there, written in the soldier's own handwriting. Signatures galore - and this activity could be done at home over the Internet. Every soldier's name was there but not all records had been scanned. A request needed to be made for a record to be made available. I made a list of names that I wanted to check and submitted my request. It took four weeks for that to happen. As I embarked on my soldier investigation, I was amazed at how much free information could be obtained about an individual person.

Once the only way to find out something about a person was to personally ask the person or find out through gossip. Not any more - publicly accessible records exist everywhere, and the Internet will yield a plethora of information if a person spends enough time searching. My friends and work colleagues were horrified at the amount of information that I was obtaining about living and long-dead people. They started to worry about their own privacy and the safety of their own identities. I started reading information about the soldiers and found it very interesting. There were often photographs of striking-looking youths. All of them being slim and athletic looking, without a trace of excess weight. In the written sections, the mates would write about the individual quirks and personalities of their regimental members. I learnt who was the joker, the serious one, the one with a volatile temper and the one who was dismissed from the army for incorrigibility. Further reading about that man indicated that he was an outright criminal who stole, forged leave documents and other documents and did many other disreputable things. The strongest wording used to describe him was incorrigible. Unfortunately, he died soon after his dismissal from the army, so he was not the one that I was looking for.

Many of the men that I researched had died during the war. As I was reading about the various soldiers and their life stories, I began to develop an affinity for the men and then I would find out about their death. This led me to become very depressed about the waste of such a lovely potential life. I started to grieve for men who had died over sixty years earlier. The whole business started making me feel very despondent. I had to give up that avenue of research before I ended up wallowing in a permanent pit of depression, so I started looking for other avenues in which to continue my search.

42. A New Tactic for Me

My work colleagues consisted of a few single women who had personal profiles on dating sites. They decided that the now-single me should be looking for a new man and I needed to have my own profile set up. I am a person who thinks outside of the square. Finding a partner was the last thing on my mind at that time as I was way too stressed and legal case focused but I thought of a way that I could utilise the site. I searched for single men who lived in the area where Wayne had his farm. I was searching to find the Will signer. There were only two men and five women listed on the site who lived in that area. I had visions of becoming a lesbian. I wrote Internet letters to the seven people using a fake ID. I was somewhat honest with the people, but not entirely, because I didn't know how well they knew the Bilks and whether they may have been friends with them or the possible Will signer. I had to be careful. I said in my letter that I was researching information for a book. I lived interstate (I made sure that my profile had me living in another Australian state). I was trying to locate a man that I knew when I was quite a bit younger who lived up in the area where he (or she depending on whether the person was male or female) lived.

I thought he (or she) looked a little like the man and maybe could have been a relative. Dating sites have people's photos so it was a feasible suggestion. I was wondering whether they would be able to help.

The people could have wondered why a person was doing her research through a dating site, but I figured that dating sites would have many odd characters, so I was merely another unusual character. I had success! A very nice young man responded and he gave me the contact details of a man he thought might be able to help me. The man gave me the details of a few possible men. I really was in another state at the time sailing, I needed to go away from time to time so that I could rest and feel safe because I never truly felt safe at home. I didn't follow up on the information because by the time I had returned home to Melbourne, some progress had occurred with my case.

43. The Case Moves a Little Forward

To have an assessment made on the genuineness of the final Will signatures it was necessary to have sample signatures (signature standards) made by Allen around the same date that the Will was signed. Fortunately for me, Allen was still signing his own cheques to pay his bills around the date of the alleged Will signing. There were many sample signatures that could be used for comparison. My lawyer had been canvassing the banks that Allen had accounts with for the original cheques that he had signed in the days and months before he had died. The banks wanted both parties to the litigation to sign the requests but there was a problem with getting Beryl to countersign the request letters. She ignored court orders and my lawyer's letters that he sent for her to sign. Many phone calls were made and letters were sent back and forth between the banks, their legal representatives and my lawyer negotiating for the cheques to be given over at my request alone, using the court orders as a reason why I had a right to them. There was a lot of to and fro negotiation between legal representatives for the banks and my lawyer.

The permission was finally given for access to the cheques. One bank required me to pay a fee but the other bank provided the cheques free of charge. These cheques, along with the Will that had the disputed signatures, were given to a forensic document examiner so he could compare the signatures. A report was made outlining anomalies between the cheque signatures and the Will signatures. The report stated that it was highly unlikely that the signatures on the cheques were made by the same person who made the signatures on the Will. I had to pay $6,600.00 for the examination and report. I finally had written proof to back up what I had been telling people all along. Thomas White-Knight, an accredited Will specialist, finally admitted to me that he had never had a Will like this one before. WOW! I told him I had always been telling him the truth. He replied that he had many people sitting in the chair where I was sitting saying similar things, but they had to provide proof before he can be sure.

After all my efforts in trying to locate the Will signer I did not follow up on the latest names that I had obtained from the dating site man because I would need to obtain recent signatures from the men and it would cost me too much money to get the writing checked. I felt that the report I now had was enough and stopped my search there. I did not know whether to ring the man back and thank him for his help anyway but thought it could end up being rather awkward so I didn't. I really enjoyed being a spy and carrying out all my spy activities. I loved looking through people's information and making up my own stories about them. I thought that I was very good at it and started to seriously think about a career change.

44. The Bilks Are Now up to Their Seventh Law Firm

It was 2011 and the new lawyers, Washingham and Partners were like a new, new, new broom. There was lots of activity happening on their side. They wanted access to everything! It was a Will case but they seemed to be turning the case into a character/de-facto property settlement/Will case. Evidence and information required for a Will case had no bearing on evidence required for a de-facto proceeding. Courts tended to take a poor view of litigants who tried to bring unrelated evidence into a case. The big problem that they had was trying to prove their claims that I was only a friend and not a relationship partner. A friend who, for the privilege of sharing Allen's house with him and no other remuneration, looked after his financial dealings, cooked his meals, cleaned the house and did the washing, ran and maintained his farms and flats, took him to all his medical visits, drove him wherever he needed to be taken since 2000 when he stopped driving, nursed him, provided him with companionship and often paid for maintenance and repairs carried out on the farm that we shared.

The first thing they wanted was access to all of Allen and my financial records that were held at Oona Macafferty's offices. I gave them permission to have access to his records but refused to let them see mine. There was nothing in my records that could have any relevance to the Will case, and it would merely give them knowledge of my financial standing. They tried to bully my lawyers into giving them access. Both my lawyers stood firm. They tried to make allegations that it took four months before they finally got to see Allen's financial documents, the implication being that it was because my lawyers took that long to give them to theirs. Washingham lawyers had been given immediate permission to see the documents but they took their time about doing it, not the other way around.

Once their lawyer had access to Allen's files she must have pored over everything with a fine-toothed comb. She found an anomaly in his bank account. The bank had made some mistakes in his monthly bank statements but I had them rectified soon as I found the mistakes. The money amounts were correct; it was the written bank statements that were incorrect. Ms. Washingham tried to imply that money was missing and demanded an explanation as to what happened to the money. I had to painstakingly draw up a table with all the dates and amounts detailed to prove that there was nothing wrong with the account. I knew that they would not find anything wrong with Allen's finances. The queries stemmed from mid-2006, when he had problems with his term deposit. In 2005, he had $1,235,000.00 in his term deposit account when he read something in the paper about his bank having some problems overseas - the bank that he had his term deposit invested in at that time. He decided that the bank could go broke so he changed banks. The new bank worked out okay at first and then started making mistakes on his monthly statements. This was the cause of the problem later for me when Ms. Washingham started examining his files.

Allen invested his money in thirty-day term deposits. Each month the bank would issue a statement showing his interest paid for that month and his latest balance. He would reinvest the deposit, along with the previous month's interest that he had earned. He never withdrew the interest, so the total amount of money that he had invested accumulated. His cash steadily increased. In mid-2006 the statements started to have errors in them. They would show that no interest was paid for the previous month, or sometimes he would have a balance of $0. I would contact the bank by telephone but they insisted on speaking to the account holder. The bank would not deal with me and I had to get Allen on the telephone, which was useless. As he couldn't hear what was being said, I had to answer the speaker's questions for him. This was easy because he kept asking the person to repeat what had been said. The speaker ended up yelling so loudly that anyone could overhear the conversation. He would tell the person at the other end of the line to speak to me on his behalf. I found it funny because the person on the phone only knew that it was a man they were speaking to; they had no way of knowing who it actually was! I felt that the person was happy to talk to me to end the frustration of trying to communicate with Allen.

Often, I had to take him into the bank to talk to the bank staff in person. This was very difficult, as he could hardly walk and he could not stand for any length of time. I had to park the car outside the door of the bank in the disabled person's parking space and queue up until it was my turn. I then had to go out to the car so I could bring him to the counter to talk with the bank staff. Whilst in the bank, which was a local branch, he signed a form giving permission for me to liaise with the bank on his behalf. This worked out fine when I was dealing with the local bank branch, but his term deposit account had been transferred to a larger branch to be handled by the people in that branch.

The representatives in the term deposit branch would not talk to me about his account. I had to ring the local branch to speak with a representative, who had to contact the term deposit branch on my behalf. There would be a three-person communication. I spoke to the term deposit branch representative via the local bank branch representative. I complained about the statements being in error and they would reassure me that the money was still there in the account, but the account number had changed so the balance on that account number was zero. Similar excuses were given as to why the interest paid was listed as a zero amount. The money amounts always worked out in the end but it was too frustrating and I pointed out to Allen that his former bank had not gone broke in the previous year and did not look like it would do so in the future. I suggested to him that he should transfer his term deposit back to the previous bank that had managed his account for many years. I rang up the personal banker representative who handled his accounts for him in the past and explained the situation to him.

Many years earlier, soon after May had died, Allen had visited the branch where his personal banker worked and introduced me to this man as his partner. It was me who liaised with this man on the telephone on his behalf from that day forward until he died. The personal banker visited him in the nursing home and arranged the transfer back to his bank. Everything seemed fine from then on. The other bank finally woke up to what had gone wrong with their handling of the account and visited him in the nursing home as well. They gave him a box of chocolates by way of an apology.

In addition to Ms. Washingham wanting to know what happened to the interest for the term deposit for the months that showed incorrect information, they also wanted to know why there were no term deposit monthly statements for the original bank during the months when his term deposit was in the other bank. Looking at the balances on the statements made it clear that Allen's entire cash was transferred into one bank when he changed banks. There was no money left in the original bank account, so there could not be any statements from that bank. They complained that a couple of bank statements for his cheque account were missing from his records. I searched for them but I could not find them. I tried contacting the bank to get copies but I was told that Beryl had already contacted them, showing the photocopy of the alleged final Will, and was now the designated bank contact who had to get the copies of the missing statements. She had to get the copies but she did not bother to do that. It was something that she could easily do but didn't, preferring to leave it to her lawyers to harass me.

I wondered whether their lawyers were careless and jumping to conclusions too quickly or if they were simply trying to be annoying by increasing the legal costs for me through all the back and forth communication. A few weeks later I went to the office of Macafferty and Co to search through my own financial records that were part of the files that were held there on my behalf. While I was searching through my own papers I found the missing bank statements for Allen's financial documents mixed in with my own bank statements. I brought this to the attention of my lawyer so that they could be passed on to Tiffany Washingham and they could then stop agitating about them being missing. I had not been keeping anything secret; they were simply misplaced and with time their whereabouts was forgotten.

Issue was then made about my running of the farms. The farm income was not enough. Why weren't there any cows bought after 2004? I had not been doing my job properly. I did not know that I was an employee! They contacted Allen's accountant to get information on wages paid to employees. There was no such information, and they were told that. He did not employ anyone to work on his farms. They also wanted his tax files and information on his livestock trading income and expenses. The accountant's files tallied with the files that they already had in his documents. He bought and sold cows when he was healthy. He was a cattle trader. In 2002, I bought many Hereford heifers and built up a herd of breeding cows. When the heifers were mature I bought a bull and bred calves to sell. I stopped regularly buying cattle. The farm income was about the same as when Allen was a cattle dealer, but it was derived in a different way. Despite the farm receipts showing that I had in fact paid for half of the cows that were bought, this fact was ignored. They started to query the cattle sale figures, ignoring the fact that half of the money belonged to me. They seemed to imply that Allen should have all the proceeds of any cattle sales. Again, it seemed to be an 'annoy the other side'- (e.g., me), cost-increasing tactic.

The next step that they took was to subpoena Allen's medical records from all his doctors. This step puzzled me; why did they want these? It would not prove capacity, I thought. I asked my doctor when next I visited him and he told me of his experience with one of his patient's medical records being subpoenaed to provide evidence of violence in that patient's relationship. He suggested that they might have wanted the medical files to find evidence of violence in our relationship. I admitted that he had hit me with his walking stick on occasions during the night when he couldn't wake me. There were notations in his nursing home files stating that he was violent and abusive towards staff and he had hit staff, but I could not figure out how this could be relevant to the case. Later, when more affidavits were sent to Thomas White-Knight, I discovered that they claimed he had been vulnerable and afraid of me since the death of his wife in 1989. They implied that I was an overbearing, controlling woman who took charge of his life and he was helpless to stand up to me. This made many people who knew the two of us laugh. They knew full well that Allen was not a man to be toyed with and I was the one who was controlled by him, not the other way around. They were willing to go to court and be witnesses for me if necessary.

When the medical records were submitted, a different story was in evidence. The medical records made many references to the benevolent care that I gave Allen and noted me as being very good to him. There was never any mention of him being afraid of me and nothing in his medical files to suggest that I ever tried to harm him. There were notations pointing out the lack of help that he received from his only daughter Beryl, who was noted as someone that he saw occasionally.

Through their lawyer they persisted with their claims that there was never a relationship between Allen and me. He was sharing a house with me out of necessity so that he could continue to live on his beloved farms and was with me for companionship only. They inserted short denigrating statements about me throughout their final affidavits. Statements that suggested he was horrified when he first learned of my claims that he was having a relationship with me and embarrassed, ashamed, etc., that people might find out that I was making these claims. These claims disgusted me. He was proud of me and our relationship. He considered me to be intelligent and attractive as well as being a nice person to live with. How could they hope to get away with such statements in a court!

In their affidavits, there was the constant suggestion that I was merely a friend who had some sort of control over Allen, and he was afraid of me. This fear control was also mentioned in the affidavit written by one of the old friends of Allen's. Beryl, Wayne and the friend of Allen's (who wrote an affidavit for the Bilks) all stated that whenever they visited with him they could tell that he wanted to speak with them privately, away from me, but I would not leave them alone. The implication was that he wanted to disclose things about his life with me and my treatment of him, but I would hover over him like a guard and never leave the room. Curiously they did not say that he confided in them whenever they telephoned or visited him while I was at work. From 2002, when he had daily carers call in to shower and care for him, a case worker managed him. The case worker regularly visited the house and talked with him about the carers he had attending to him and how he was living in general. Each year she made an annual assessment of his condition and care needs.

During this visit his case worker filled in a tick-the-box report which also contained handwritten notes based on the answers that she was given. Allen was required to sign the completed report. For the report, he answered questions about his living situation, including who he lived with and the relationship he had with this person. He always said that he lived with a partner and named me as his partner. I always arranged for the caseworker and any other people that he knew to visit him while I was at work to give him more and varied social contact. By then he had reached a stage where he was extremely disinclined to go out and socialise. He was embarrassed by his appearance as he had become hunched over and wizened looking. He was no longer the attractive man that he once was. He dribbled a lot and he could not eat anything without spilling his food all over himself. The case worker made her home visits to him during the day while I was at work. It was always a friendly visit, where she sat with him and had a chat over a cup of tea or coffee. There was no one telling him what to say or not say. I was not standing over him guarding him, and I could not remotely control him. If he had any fears for his safety, he would have been able to tell this person in confidence. Although he had ample opportunity to state his situation, there was never any written record made of him confiding that he was unhappy in his life with me or that he considered me to be anything less than a devoted, caring partner to him.

Medical records obtained from his other treating doctors also stated that he had a partner. His initial consultation with his urologist for his prostate surgery in 1990 stated that he had a girlfriend and sexual function was normal. The girlfriend at that time was me. There were numerous references to me, his partner, throughout all his medical records. In a consult with Dr. Dendrite a couple of years before he died, Dr. Dendrite noted in his file that Allen discussed the possibility of him having more children with me.

The same discussion was penned in a letter from Dr. Dendrite to Allen's GP. I did not think that his medical records helped them with their case in any way.

On 4th May 2011 Washinghams submitted the final affidavit material from their clients and from their witnesses, the Dauntons. There were now three sets of affidavits from the Bilks, the Dauntons and Neville McNaughton. In addition, there were affidavits from four new witnesses: one from a friend of Beryl's; two from two separate old acquaintances of Allen's and one from Beryl's aunt, May's sister. She had signed hers in August 2007, when she was 88 years old, but for some reason it was not submitted until 2011. That was four years later!

The affidavit of Ralph Daunton had been expanded from six points of information in the first one to twenty-five points of information. In the latest affidavit, he went into the historical aspects about how he met Beryl and Wayne and of his friendship with them over the years, leading on to how he met Allen and May. In this final affidavit, he stated that he watched Allen sign every page of the Will slowly and carefully. He wrote about the time that it took him to sign each page of his Will. He stated that he signed gradually and took quite a bit of time to do it. He described how he had his right hand placed flat on the paper while signing and he moved the pen across the page. It asserted that he was not assisted with the signing. I was most surprised at this statement, as I was extremely familiar with the method that Allen used to sign documents. His hand position was always the other way up. His muscle control was virtually non-existent so he could not hold his hand flat on the paper while holding a pen. He rested the back of his hand and his knuckles on the paper and had his fingers pointed towards his body while he was clutching the pen. He held his hand somewhat similar to the way many left-handed people write, except he was using his right hand. This person's description of the Will signer did not match a description of what Allen looked like when he was signing documents.

Steven Daunton, Ralph's son, the other witness, had never met Allen before. His 2011 affidavit was only slightly expanded on the previous ones. There was one major exception between the earlier affidavits and the 2011 affidavit, and that was the statement about the date on the Will. In the 2010 affidavits he wrote something about his father asking him the date with him suggesting that he thought the date was the 25th of February. He implied that he now remembers that the date was really the 26th of February because he was told by someone that was the date that the Will was signed. The latest affidavit lacked a statement that was in the 2010 affidavit of Steven Daunton, namely, that he was out driving with his father in his car when Wayne called them on the mobile phone. He asked them whether they could come and witness his father-in-law sign a Will. It seemed bizarre to me that they were signing a very important document and they made it clear that they had a mobile phone, yet no one checked the phone to ensure that they had the correct date!

All four witnesses to the Will signing, the Bilks and Ralph Daunton and Steven Daunton, blamed Steven for giving them the incorrect date to write on the Will. Steven wrote that he thought the date was February 25th. Ralph claimed that he checked the calendar because he was advised that the date was the 26th February, not the 25th February, and he was now sure that he had originally written the wrong date based on the advice that he was given and that the correct date was Sunday the 26th February. Steven was taking the bullet for everyone getting the date wrong on the Will.

My personal perception based on the description made of Alan's appearance in the affidavits was that there could have been a will signed by an old appearing man on the 25th but Thomas claimed that my conspiracy theory would not wash in the court so I said nothing further on the matter.

45. Proving Allen's Lack of Mental Lucidity

Both Ralph and Steven Daunton attested to the fact that Allen was perfectly lucid and although he appeared frail, he looked quite healthy! At around this time in his nursing home notes the information was very much different. The following notations were made by me based on conversations with the nursing home staff about his wellbeing:

January 3rd, 2007 I was told that Allen's behaviour was very unusual and he was very confused during that day. His speech was impaired and he was slow to respond to questions. He could only verbalise two or three words at a time and could not speak in full sentences. His comprehension and awareness of the things happening around him fluctuated throughout the day and it took a lot of time for him to assimilate information. He was not able to initiate or carry out daily living activities. I was told by the staff that he is emotionally dependent on me, his partner. The nursing home often needed to contact me by telephone when I wasn't there so that he could talk to me. He could not hear me on the phone but the staff could relay the conversations between us. One of the nursing staff told me when I arrived that Allen had decided that the goats on the farm had escaped and they were in the animal pound. The nurse told me that Allen wanted her to ring me so she pretended to ring and then told Allen, "It's OK, Catherine has taken the goats to the market to be milked." Allen replied, "Oh! Good." He was happy with that. The funny thing was Allen knew that I never milked the goats. They had kids and the kids drank their milk.

He was anxious and confused about his ability to pay the nursing home bill and worried about his medications being given at the right times of the day. He was also confused about what time it was and where he was on a daily basis. This was a very evident theme throughout recorded conversations that we had. I made the recordings because my lawyer suggested that I should tape a few our conversations to give an indication to others of his cognitive state at that stage of his illness. To make it legally useable evidence I had to make it known to Allen that I was making a tape recording of our conversations. I did this and clearly placed the tape recorder on a table in front of him so that he could see it. He never commented or told me not to do it. He did not pay any attention to the recorder at all.

As evidenced by the recordings he often diverged onto tangents during conversations. His responses often did not match what was being said to him.

The next few paragraphs are transcripts of conversations between us taped by me in November 2006. The first occurred one evening in the nursing home during a visit with him. I had just entered his room. He looked at me and said. "Catherine, it's not 6 o'clock is it?" "No, It's seven." "This clock is wrong." I replied referring to the clock that was on the dresser beside his bed. "What have you been doing?" He asked me. "I've been home and had some tea. Now I've come to see you.. I brought you some cake and a banana." I told him while handing him the piece of cake that I had for him. "What's this?" He asked. "It is some chocolate cake that I made for you and a banana". "What was I going to say?" "Oh, I remember, on Friday, you've got your doctor's appointment at 11.00. Do you want me to try and get you into the dentist at about 9.00 or will I try and get you in to the dentist on Saturday?" Allen interjected, "I'm sorry, but a..." "I... they haven't given me any pills." "I'm sure that they have." I responded. "What...?" he said. "You would have just had one a little while ago." I told him. "Really?" "I'll go and check if you want." "I've taken one, have I?" he asked me. "Mmm, about an hour ago you would have had one." He then asked me, "Am I going to the cow sale tomorrow?" I told him "No, you said you wanted to go to the dentist. Will I make you an appointment?" He answered, "See the lady that's there?" he was referring to one of the staff members who was walking past the door. I said, "Yep." He started to tell me but changed the topic mid sentence, "She's good that one well look, I'm just not feeling well now." I asked him, "Why? What is wrong?" He replied "Why? Ohh. Oh Beryl came down, err, last night–no..." "Did she?" "Was it today?" He asked me. "Today?" I queried. He said, "Yes." "Maybe it was the night before." I had no idea if she had visited him so I said, "OK.". Allen then asked me, "Did she come here?" I suggested to him, "I think she did, yes, maybe a couple of days ago. I don't know." He muttered back to me, "Well, if she did come, and I don't know... You don't know where my, err, I don't know." He continued, "She came and we talked about things and I know everything about you know and I told her that's what I know, you know. Do you think I'm just--I don't know?" "Well, I don't know either" I responded. I did not get him to the dentist on the next day but fortunately the dentist had a light workload one day during the following week and he attended to Allen in the nursing home.

Then I recalled that he had telephoned her on the previous weekend while he was at the farm with me, "Well, you rang her up on Saturday. Do you remember that?" "You were here when she came." He told me. "No, I wasn't." "It must have been one of her kids then." He stated. "You rang her on Saturday." "I rang her today, did I? He asked. "You rang her Saturday. I don't know about today. I told him. "On Monday?" he said. The conversation ended here because Allen suddenly fell asleep.

Conversation between Allen and me at home on the farm October 2006We were in the lounge room going over his bills. I was showing him the invoices and getting him to sign the cheques. These I had prewritten to save him from spending too much time trying to think about them and becoming stressed. "That's the Hospital for $3,000 (It was the monthly bill for the Nursing Home)." He rambled on while trying to sign the cheque. "Well, that's--I tell you what it's funny, out there they're not allowed, the fellow who mops the floor. It's the same with the black fellow; he says, 'Hello Allen.' He brought that black fellow here, he did, and he went through the house, he did. I asked him, "What did he do in the house?" He replied, "You know, it's queer the way they handle it; it's private." "You know they have had two inspections in the last month." I presumed that he was talking about the nursing home because we were paying the bill and it was on his mind.

After we had finished doing the bookwork I thought a change would be good for him so I asked him, "Do you want to go for a drive down the paddock now? "AL said, "What?" I repeated, "Do you want to go for a drive down the paddock?" He asked, "What is the time now?" "Three." I told him. "It's three o'clock now? You'll have to get me ready." Allen used the power button on his lifting chair to get himself into a standing position and tried to put on his jacket. "This is upside down or some bloody thing." I was putting the papers and paraphernalia away while he struggled to put his arm into the sleeve of his jacket. "It's not. It is the right way up. If you wait for a minute I will help you." I told him. He dropped his jacket on the floor and looked around the room. "Is there anything else I haven't got? A hat, have I?" "It is in the car." I told him. "Where's the car? He asked. "Out the back where we left it? I replied. "Where's out the back?" He asked.

We finally get into the car when Al falls asleep. A short while later as I am driving him back to the nursing home he wakes up. He looks out the window and states, "Look at that there, a Plane tree or something!" It was a power pole that he was looking at. He rambled on. "You know one thing they haven't put in with land the price it is, I don't know why a golf course…. there you are once again, Johnny Lee. Lee is a smart bugger; he… a golf course he… get in for a golf course. There's one thing about the…. it takes a lot of land to put it in. He was talking about a friend that he had over twenty years ago. He sold his farm and it was turned into a golf course. I stated, "But not everybody wants a golf course." "This tree is too close to their driveway" he replied. He was looking at a tiny shrub growing beside someone's driveway. I was about to say something but he interjected with, "Oh look, there's a cow in there, in that garage!" "I don't understand you; there's a what?" I said. He continued, "Well, they can certainly grow the grass. I know what it needs is a shower of rain on it." I think he was talking about the grass growing on the nature strip by the nursing home driveway. I was not sure. I parked the car in the car park and took him inside the home.

Conversation between Allen and me one Monday evening in the nursing home, late November 2006. Allen said, "You're here! I'm talking to Beryl, did she come here last night?" "Probably" I replied, "But she wasn't here when I was with you." Allen persisted, "Last night--did she come here last night?" "She might have come here last night." I told him. "What?" "She might have come here last night." I repeated. "Where's my hearing aid? He asked. "I'm trying to get it fixed." I told him. "Where is it?" He asked again. "It's in the car. I'm trying to get it fixed." I replied. It was not working again! He queried me, "In the car?" "Yes." I told him. "I'm going to try and take it somewhere tomorrow." "Yes." He said. He continued with, "The cows need worming. Are you going to worm them today?" "It is too dark. It is night time. We'll leave them for now." I told him. His bed was beside a window and it was dark outside but it did not register in Al's mind that it was night time.

"What? Why not?" He persisted. "Let's leave them for now. We could do them on the weekend" I suggested. He responded with, "You don't know what's happening? You don't want to marry me, do you?" I could see a lot of problems arising from such a union at this late stage of our relationship. "I think you've left it too late." I said. "Where are you going now….school?" "No, I'm going home after I leave here. I'm going to bed." I told him. He asked me again, "Are you going to work?" I repeated, "I'm going home. I'm going to bed. I am very tired." Tired? He said. "Yes." I replied, "I am going to the farm." "Tired?" he repeated again. "Yes, I am going to the farm." "Are you?" He asked. He continued, "Well, what day is this?" "Monday." I told him. "Are you thinking of going to school?" He inquired. "I've been there all day. It's night time. It's dark." He didn't respond. He was off on another tangent. "Oooh. I was surprised. I looked at some of those cattle earlier today; they were a bit better than I thought they'd be. I think you are crazy not to sell. There's a lot of money there; they'll go backwards. We'll only sell the good ones, you know. You don't agree with me?" I told him, "We have been selling them. I'm going to sell some more soon." "Are you? He asked. "Yes, but I haven't had time lately." I had sold some young cattle two weeks previously but I was busy writing student reports over the past week, a thing that is very stressful for me and I could not spare the time to send cows to the market during that week. "If we've been selling, I don't know." He stated. "You do know." I assured him. He responded with a question. "Have I had any breakfast?" The cow conversation was out of his mind. "Yes." "Am I going to have a bath?" The staff usually showered him in the mornings after breakfast. "Yes, and they will put your jamas on you." "Well, what have you done about getting pills for tonight and tomorrow?" He asked. "They have got lots of pills here." I reassured him. "Who has?" "Here, the nurses here, they've got lots of them." "Does she know about it?" He asked me. "Yes." I assured him. "It's under control, have you?" he asked. "Yes." He wanted more reassurance. "You've told them, have you?" "Yes, I've told them." Satisfied with my responses he immediately fell asleep.

In Allen's nursing home file, there are numerous notes relating to his concerns about being able to pay the monthly bill. His monthly income from his investments was about thirteen thousand dollars and he had one million three hundred thousand dollars in a term deposit. In

2006 there were problems with the account on a few occasions; the monthly statement did not credit any interest to his cheque account and the monthly statement showed a zero balance. These issues did not concern Allen in the slightest and they had to be dealt with by me, but his nursing home bill seemed to worry him.

Notes made about Allen's health in the last few weeks of his life.

4th January Allen has a chest infection, confusion, sweating, shaking.

3/1/07; 16/1/07; 24/1/07 He had urinary tract infections.

12/1/07 He had a wheezy cough and was put on Ventolin nebuliser.

14/1/07 He was unwell and incontinent; he also had swallowing problems.

20/1/07 He was in pain and had bruised ribs from flopping over against the armrest of his chair. His concentration was impaired.

21st January Nursing home staff discussed Terminal Care Wishes with me. Sadly, I told them of Allen's wishes to be buried at Kew Cemetery.

25th January He was shivering the same way that he shivered back in the 1980s before he went onto medication; he had difficulty with taking his tablets.

3rd February Allen was wheelchair bound.

8th February He was hallucinating.

10th February He was confused and sweating. He spent the day resting in bed.

11th February He was anxious and agitated during the day. He spent this day resting in bed.

11/2/07 until 10/3/07 He was being treated for pressure sores.

12th February He could attend social functions as a passive observer only and could not actively participate in any social activity. His medical condition had declined.

14th to the 17th February He was unwell and he spent these days resting in bed. He was becoming semi-vegetative. His treating physician's notes stated that it was clear that he would not live for much longer.

21st until 25th February He was unwell and he spent these days resting in bed.

His Speech Pathologist examined him in February 2007 and stated that he could only follow simple spoken instructions. He imitated oral movements but could not vocalize his expression and his ability to signal for help were all impaired. He was also confused about what was happening around him and displayed inappropriate responses. His eating and swallowing abilities were impaired. Around this time Beryl was emailing Carlita Vargos, claiming him to be very with it and very on the ball.

Reading the nursing home notes on Alan's final days strengthened my conviction that Ralph and Steven Daunton did not witness Allen sign the 2007 Will on 26th Feb, but they witnessed someone claiming to be him sign a Will on 25th Feb 2007. Ralph Daunton had not seen him in over two years and over the previous fifteen or so years, I had never recalled Allen meeting with him or even mentioning him. From 2000 onwards he could not drive a car and had to be driven by me everywhere, including to social functions with the Bilks. I had never met Ralph or Steven Daunton. I did not accompany him to one Christmas function with them in 2003, which is when Ralph stated to have last seen Allen prior to witnessing the Will signing. Memories of people that you only have very occasional contact with are not that clear, especially when a person's physical appearance changes a lot, such as Allen's had in the last couple of years of his life. I doubted that Ralph would have such a clear memory of him, and an old man of similar build sitting in a wheelchair in a darkened room could easily pass himself off as Allen. Ralph stated in his affidavit that Allen was in the old part of the house when he visited to witness the signing. This part of the house is dark and dingy, with small windows and poor lighting.

46. If You Throw Enough Mud at a Wall, some of it May Stick

I had to endure a considerable number of denigrating statements being made against me in the affidavits that were written by the plaintiff and her friends. A neighbour made the comment to me, "They are trying to say so many bad things about you that it will affect people's thinking. The saying goes, 'If you throw enough mud at a wall some of it will stick.' The more awful things that they say about you the more likely it will be that some things are going to be believed." While Allen lived in the house with me before he went into the nursing home, an overriding theme in the affidavits purported that the state of the house that he had to live in was deplorable and so was his physical state. It was claimed that the house was very dirty and that he was unkempt and dishevelled in appearance, the implication being that it was my fault.

The claims did not take into account that from 1999 onwards three different women came to the house each day to attend to his needs. The women cleaned up after him while I was at work and did his washing, made his bed and fed him. They were responsible for his showering and keeping him clean and tidy. If it was felt that he was not being adequately cared for, no comment was ever made while he was alive. They could have made a complaint to the Government department responsible for his casual in-house carers but they didn't. I was the only person who interacted with the case worker, and I would address any concerns with her, and she would then arrange to rectify any problems associated with his daily care. Other visitors to the house did not contact anyone with any concerns about him or the state of his living situation. It seems that these issues only became noted years after he had died. Obviously, they did not think his living situation was very grim while he was alive.

Another claim made against me was how I snuck him into the nursing home behind everyone's back and didn't tell his daughter or family that I was doing it. Claims were also made against me that I never informed the nursing home staff that he had a daughter and grandchildren. According to Beryl in her affidavit, when she finally found her father, the staff that worked in the nursing home was amazed to find out that he had a daughter and grandchildren. Allen, however, was quite capable of telling people about his family situation when he first went to live in the nursing home. When someone intends to be deceptive in important legal documents, the person should be very careful that the deception cannot be proven. Fortunately for me, when I read these claims it was with great delight that I realised that I had evidence to prove that the affidavit claims were completely incorrect.

I throw very little out. I don't consider myself a hoarder; I like to call myself 'An Accumulator'. Papers, receipts and documents were stored in metal filing cabinets in a shed on the property. I never deliberately hoard the stuff; it simply accumulates as more and more is added to the filing cabinet without me getting around to sorting through and disposing of papers that are too old or no longer needed. More important papers were kept in the offices of Macafferty and Co. I gleefully skipped out to my shed and looked through the filing cabinets where I stored my miscellaneous papers. I had copies of telephone accounts that listed telephone numbers called, with the length of time that was spent on the call. Beryl's number was on an account, indicating that a call was made to her on the morning that her father went into the nursing home. There was also a call made on the following weekend, when I took him home to the farms for the day and he talked with her for twenty-four minutes. He made another call to her number about an hour later, when he talked for another nine minutes. It would have been impossible for him to talk with her for this length of time on the phone and not mention anything about the nursing home. The impending move to the home was the sole reason that he telephoned her in the first place. She knew exactly where he was going and when. I had evidence that the home knew about her because her contact details were listed on the application and admissions forms. I had the original copies handwritten by me stored in my shed filing cabinet. When I first took him into the home I told the staff about the members of his family, including his daughter; this was noted in his file as well.

Despite all my evidence I was still quite miffed at the implication that it was my responsibility to tell the nursing staff about Allen's family situation. The home had numerous people working there, as it was a high care facility. The place was staffed twenty-four hours a day, seven days a week. The staff there worked in shifts on rotating rosters. They also rotated through the various wings of the home. It would have been impossible for me to have met every staff member and told them all the details of his background. He was the person interacting with the staff every day and at the time of his entry into residential care, he was quite capable of telling everyone about the individual members of his family and their relationship to him. I felt that the implication that he was incapable of doing this in 2005 was counter to their claims that in 2007 he was perfectly lucid and could recognize people that he had rarely seen in the past. He could call people when he wanted; it was not a jail. He had a mobile telephone with him that had telephone numbers that he wanted stored in the memory. He was incapable of dialling a telephone number himself but he could get a staff member to dial for him. He rang me on many occasions like this, and I am sure that he also rang his daughter.

With serendipitous delight, I rummaged through my shed, finding files, receipts and scrappy notes to prove inaccuracies in the Bilk's and their friend's affidavits. One friend of theirs who wrote an affidavit for them claimed that he had telephoned me in January 2010 saying that he had only just found out about Allen's death. He already knew well before this time because he had telephoned my home in January 2008, when my mother was staying with me. My mother had been a legal secretary in her working life and she always kept good records. She wrote this person's name, number and details on a dated telephone message notepad. I filed the note in my filing cabinet under Telephone numbers and Addresses, along with other notes containing people's telephone numbers and addresses. In this person's affidavit, he stated that he was a very long term good friend of Allen and Beryl and had a very close relationship with them when they lived in May's Brighton home. He was not informed of Allen's death and was very upset to hear of it when he first found out upon contact with Beryl in 2010.

The fact that he knew about his death in 2008, evidenced by my mother's note, made it appear that the other denigrating statements that he made might not be entirely true. In his affidavit, there were comments about the poor state of cleanliness of the house and Allen's dishevelled appearance. It was asserted that I tried to prevent him from having contact with him and he even wrote alleged telephone conversations that he claimed to have had with me, where he declared that I said to him things like, "Oh no, it's the nuisance man ringing again!" and "It is too much bother for me to help (Allen) talk with you all the time. Don't ring here anymore; he can't hear you on the phone anyway." These are conversations that I would have never said to him or to anyone else. I would not even be that rude to the telemarketing callers that regularly rang and certainly would not have said such things to a friend of Allen's. I felt that they needed a new script writer when I read some parts of this person's affidavit. He wrote, about 2005 I rang Allen on the telephone where he told me, "She's forcing me to go into a nursing home. I don't need to go to one of those places. I am not sick." The friend wrote that Allen was whispering and he thought that it was because he had lost his voice but then he heard a sound in the background. It was a squeaking noise like a door that had hinge that needed oiling being closed and he realised that Allen was secretly ringing him. He could hear the sound of a door clicking shut and Allen whispering conspiratorially, "I have to hang up now before she finds out that I am ringing you. If I can I will try to ring you and tell you where I am. I am not sure that I will be able to do it." That was the last time that I ever heard from my very good friend. I did not know that the nursing home that he went into was in the next street from where I lived.

Throughout the affidavits sent on behalf of the Bilks there seemed to be an underlying theme of things being overheard in the background of telephone conversations. This witness even went so far as to compare the state of the house where Allen and I lived to the house where he lived with May, claiming that he was now living in accommodations that were of a far inferior standard to the house he lived in with his wife. He stated that he was horrified at the state of the house that poor Allen was living in. It was a very dirty house with dirty clothes and dishes left lying around the house. Poor Allen had no food to eat. The toilet was filthy. The friend had scoured the cups and the teapot for poor Allen so that they could have a cup of tea.

    In fact, we did not have a teapot because we used tea bags! We had a dishwasher in the house so there could not have been too many dirty dishes lying around. This man should have checked his facts before writing. I maintained the house where we lived and regularly painted it and carried out repairs. The other house where he lived when May was alive, was filled with cats that had nasal congestion and bowel incontinence issues. There were many feline bodily fluid accidents occurring in that house. It has been unoccupied since her death in 1989 and it is still unoccupied. I seriously wondered how such a witness would be able to successfully stand up in court and back up his claims under cross examination.

47. The Making of the Final Will Explained

I felt that the most amazing affidavits were the ones written by Neville McNaughton. After the introductory paragraph giving information about his background, qualifications and association with Wayne Bilk, the next paragraph said that he had a phone call from Wayne asking him if he could write a Will for his father-in-law. He told him okay, he could do it for him. He wrote that Wayne told him in the telephone conversation that Allen wanted a clause in the Will that would give me nothing if I did not settle my court case before he died, and that Allen had a hearing problem so he could not talk to him on the phone personally. Therefore, Wayne would dictate the contents of the Will to him. Because of the hearing problem he felt that it was okay for Wayne to tell him what to put in the Will instead of Allen. He thought that he could hear Allen speaking in the background of the telephone conversation because he heard other voices talking in the background. Oh! The scriptwriter is at it again! Something is heard in the background of a telephone conversation! He did not explain how he knew what Allen's voice would have sounded like, considering he had never met him or spoken to him on a telephone.

In a later affidavit Neville McNaughton stated as it was such an uncomplicated Will to write, he did not feel that it was necessary for him to drive the distance to the nursing home to meet with Allen in person. He stated, "I wrote down Wayne's information that he wanted included in the Will on an A4 notepad, including the clause preventing her from getting any of the estate if she didn't settle her case against Allen." His next statement went as follows: "I opened a computer file on my computer. I made a cover sheet and a new case number." He then went on to state in his affidavit, "I can no longer find any evidence to show that I had made the Will." The documents related to the making of the Will seemed to have been lost, and he did not have any other documents about it. Neville McNaughton never met Allen and did not ever speak to him. The original Will-making files have been lost, so there is no record of the exact date when the Will was made. The dates noted on the affidavit are very vague: 'about this time', etc., - and the vague times changed between the affidavits. One affidavit stated that he made the Will in November; another affidavit stated that it was in February. One could imagine a lawyer could lose files or information over the years, but this lawyer lost his entire Will making files, both the handwritten and the computer saved notations, in a period of two months!

In addition, Wayne failed to provide any telephone bills to prove dates and times when he made the calls to Neville McNaughton, nor could he prove that he did in fact make the call from the nursing home. Telephone companies hold their records for seven years so it was quite possible for Wayne to obtain copies of old telephone bills to help his case, but he didn't. What I and other people who read Neville McNaughton's affidavits found quite puzzling was the fact that there are at least twenty law firms within three kilometres of the nursing home and at least forty more within a twelve-kilometre distance. Wayne chose a lawyer who was located over sixty kilometres away. If Allen genuinely wanted to make a new Will with another lawyer and keep it secret from me, as was claimed, then they could have easily got someone local to come and see him in person. If that was not possible, then Wayne could have driven him to his lawyer friend's office to make the new Will. Their claims of his good health during his visits to their home on both the 18th and the 26th meant that he surely would have been well enough to go to McNaughton's office in the month or months prior to these dates. It seemed clear that the new Will was not Allen's intentions. That is why the person who was a friend of Wayne's was used. Any other lawyer who did not know Wayne would have had grave concerns about making a Will via the telephone for another person.

48. Catherine the Accumulator Finds Evidence to Prove the Lies

Beryl made a very brief first affidavit, followed by a final lengthy one, that focussed on debunking the relationship issue. In her unsworn affidavit, she had written about her father being most concerned about his relationship with me. In her sworn version of the 2009 affidavit she had deleted all mention of him having any relationship with me.

In conversations with Allen during the 80s and 90s Wayne often boasted to him about how he handled his business dealings. He worked on the principle that he could get away with a lot of things because people could not prove the accuracy of what was being said. He boasted about an early employer of his who was in court over a tax issue. He was impressed with the way that this man misled the judge and the other side's legal representation. He didn't lie; he simply made deceptive statements that gave the listener the wrong impression. I felt that was what was happening in the affidavits that had been presented. An overriding theme throughout the affidavits was that Carlita Vargos had a friendship with me through our dog breeding and training clubs, where they claimed we were both members. Perhaps, during their visits to Carlita's office the dog breeding and training discussion may have occurred with Beryl and Wayne, like the one that she had with Allen and me. Wayne was very fond of dogs and always had one that he took with him in his car everywhere that he went. There are dog breeding and dog training clubs throughout Victoria and there is a major conglomeration of clubs around the outer suburbs of Melbourne. The dog club that Carlita was a member of was 20 kilometres away from the one that I was a member of.

In Beryl's final affidavit she precisely noted the name of the dog club and the year (1999 in one affidavit and 2001 in another) in which she alleges that I was a member of that exact kennel club branch along with Carlita. They were making serious allegations against the integrity of Carlita, who always acted on Allen's behalf, with the highest ethical standard. They were relying on records not being available because official records are not usually kept for more than seven years, however, they did not count on me and my accumulating habits! I was not sure whether the kennel club headquarters kept records for longer than seven years. I thought that they might, due to the possibility of dog bites and dog attacks happening during meetings, but my kennel club branch did not have any records going back that far. I did and I virtually did cartwheels from my house to the shed in my excitement to get papers that were filed under Dog breeding/dog training Club. There I had detailed members' lists for the years 1999 to 2004. Every member of my kennel club branch was listed, with their name, contact details, car registration, and dog's name, breed and colour. Not one list had Carlita's name on it! I also had copies of my kennel club's monthly newsletters and various other documents. Her name was never mentioned and she was not a member!

When Thomas White-Knight first informed me about receiving the final affidavits he sounded very grave. My heart stopped beating momentarily. If he sounded worried, then I had a problem. I drove to his office immediately to collect my copies. He told me in a serious voice that the affidavits were filled with minutiae not at all relevant to our case. I asked him if we were going to ignore it but he said, 'No!' 'We will need to address the issues because it slanders your character it will be a case of who is believed. After I returned to his office a week later with my responses and associated evidence he seemed perplexed by my smug smile and gleeful appearance. His dire look changed to astonished amazement as I produced evidence addressing every incorrect and denigrating statement in Beryl's affidavit. He seemed most impressed. I felt that this was one instance where accumulating paid off. After 2004 the kennel club stopped sending out detailed membership information due to changes in privacy regulations. It was fortunate for me that I had retained my earlier records even though the information was not used in my affidavit, as Thomas said it was not relevant for my case but it would be kept on file should it be required. He felt that the case was being bogged down with minute issues but if they had to be addressed he was pleased that I had evidence to support my rebuttal of the claims that had been made. I had never met Carlita prior to Allen engaging her as his legal representative.

In June 2011 Beryl engaged a neurologist to read the nursing home reports and all the affidavits from both sides to write a report on Allen's cognitive capacity at the time of the alleged last Will signing. The neurologist submitted his curriculum vitae that consisted of seven pages. I presumed that this was to dazzle everyone with his importance to cover his lack of background knowledge about Allen. He had never met him! His resume was followed by a just over one-page long report on Allen's capacity. He based his report on what was written in the affidavits of Wayne and Beryl's friends. He stated it was because they were not going to obtain any benefit from the estate. Based on what these friends had written, he formed the opinion that Allen would have been perfectly capable of understanding what he was doing on the day that he allegedly approved the Will and on the day that he signed it. He suggested that he could have been pretending to be unable to understand Carlita when she visited him in the nursing home on 16 February 2007 and formed the opinion that he no longer had capacity.

I had Allen's treating physician for the nursing home write a report, but the neurologist stated that although both the doctor and the nursing home notes noted chest infections and general poor health on the days around the 26th there was nothing to say that he was unwell on the 26th so the affidavits of the friends would appear to be correct in that he was most likely to be mentally aware on that day. He ignored my affidavit because I stood to gain from the process. Carlita's affidavit was ignored because he read in the opposing affidavits that Allen did not like Carlita anymore. Allen's treating physician's report was ignored because when he wrote it in 2011 he noted that he did not remember Allen clearly and based his report on his and the nursing home's notes from 2007, when he was personally treating him. The physician wrote his report four years after Allen's death and he was being honest. I felt aggrieved that a prominent medical practitioner could make a legal assessment on a person that he had never met based on lay people's observations made during short meetings with him prior to his death. I seriously doubted that the person whom they met and were writing about was even Allen. The fact that he considered these people's opinions more accurate than the nursing home staff notes and those of his treating physician seemed incredulous to me.

His physician was still was a person who had observed him first-hand when he visited him in the nursing home, so his medical file notes made during these visits to treat him would have been very accurate.

Beryl got this same neurologist to write a further affidavit report on handwriting. He explained the changes that can occur in a person's handwriting due to Parkinson's disease. He made some comparisons between the signatures on earlier Wills signed by Allen and the final Will. He refused to comment on whether the signatures were made by the same person and suggested that an examination needed to be done by a professional document examiner.

Other evidence was submitted including an item that came from the offices of Tibor Norwich - the letter that Wayne had written to Carlita wanting a new Will drawn up in November 2006. The other item was a diary that Wayne kept. The diary had a notation for February 1st and was written in rough note form detailing the new Will distribution amounts. The rest of the diary was sealed with bulldog clips holding the other pages firmly closed and inaccessible. Thomas White-Knight, who inspected the diary at Tiffany Washingham's office, was forbidden to see any other pages. He felt that if the diary had one entry about making a new Will, then surely other pages would have entries of dates and times relevant to the Will making and signing, particularly as the various affidavits were very vague as to the date when it was decided that the new Will was to be written and the Will making files were lost. The stated dates varied from sometime between November 2006 and February 2007. That fact, along with the fact that the Will making records were lost, meant that information contained in such a diary could be vital. The diary was subpoenaed, but its production was objected to and it was never submitted to the court.

I found the diary very interesting when I studied the handwritten notations in the pages that we were permitted to view. It seemed that the notations in the diary had more than likely been written by different people. The writing in a few entries had a similar appearing letter 's' to the letter 's' in the 2007 Will signature, and when I photocopied these examples onto clear overhead projector transparency sheets and superimposed them over the letter 's' in the Will signatures, they were exact copies. I knew that Allen had not written in that diary but the person who had, wrote in a similar manner to the signature on the Will. I had the handwriting in the diary and several other handwriting samples of Wayne's checked by the document examiner, but it was declared that the signature on the Will was not Wayne's handwriting. The identity of the person whose writing in the diary was similar to the writing in the Will would never be known. It would be necessary to access other pages in the diary for more handwriting samples and the costs of investigation would be too high, so it was decided to leave the matter alone.

49. Mediation Number Four: The Final One

The final mediation was to be held four weeks before we were due to go to trial. Tiffany Washingham was trying to get an extension of time. They wanted the trial date to be postponed. The request was denied. The case had already been dragged out for more than four years. The mediation day arrived. I attended with my son and daughter-in-law, both of my lawyers, Thomas White-Knight and Oona Macafferty, our barrister and a young woman trainee. My side had seven members. The other side had more people. It was a case of 'there are more of us than there are of you. We are the more powerful side!' Ms. Washingham could not decide which woman was me out of the four women who were present. She mistakenly guessed it was Oona Macafferty, who was very offended. She thought Ms. Washingham should have recognised her as a colleague.

We all trooped into the room for the mediation. I was shocked at Beryl's appearance. Her face was heavily lined and pinched looking. Her mouth was pursed and had wrinkled lines radiating out from her lips, like the lines around a smoker's lips, but she didn't smoke. There was no sign of Wayne and everyone on my team wondered why he was absent. In the past, he had always been actively fighting alongside his wife. I had to endure the intense scrutiny of the entire gang. I was stared at by all of them. Although I was becoming accustomed to the staring from representatives of the other camp, now I wished I had brought some fake horns to wear just to make them feel that I really was a devil. I felt sure that they all thought that I looked too good to have not been in a relationship with Allen when we lived together. I wondered if they felt that there would be a problem convincing a court that Allen felt embarrassed that people might think that he was having a relationship with me. I looked at their faces and thought that they looked doubtful about whether they believed the claims about me were true. One lawyer stared at me the whole time. Another lawyer kept looking at me and shaking his head from side to side. Another pair looked at me then looked at each other and rolled their eyes at each other. Needless to say, despite the way that I looked, no settlement was reached on that day. Negotiations continued between both sets of lawyers the next day. Tiffany Washingham wanted the trial date cancelled, as they felt that a settlement could be reached. The trial date had taken too long to reach and my side refused to cancel the trial date. The clock was ticking!

50. Fighting Back

My objections to the grant of probate were lack of knowledge and capacity, and the document that was being purported to be his Will was never intended by Allen to be his Will. The Will case was supposed to be based solely on these issues. Instead, it appeared to have changed to include relationship, character and financial issues.

I had to address the relationship and character issues. I asked friends, relatives, work colleagues and neighbours if they would be prepared to make statements on my behalf. In all, I prepared a list of fifty people who could give evidence supporting my claims that Allen and I were assuredly in a relationship and socialised as a couple; that I provided excellent care for him; that I did not bully, harass or mistreat him and that we lived together in a clean, respectable home. During the years of his illness he had told many of the witnesses that I was the most important person in his life and he was still living only because of the way that I cared for him.

The court date was looming so my lawyer started making final preparations. He selected ten people from my list that he wished to interview for affidavit statements. They were close friends, neighbours and business associates of ours. He got me to set up a timetable for my relationship witnesses to come to my place on the Friday before the first day of the court case as he wanted to talk with them and make affidavits for them to sign. The court case was scheduled to start on the Monday following the witness interviewing day. The purpose was to show to the judge at the beginning of the trial that a relationship did exist as this would save court time arguing over an issue that was not relevant to the case. It took me some hours to set up the meetings, but I managed to get it all ready for him. After Beryl and I agreed on a settlement I had to call everyone again to cancel the meetings.

In her final affidavit Beryl complained that she only received property and money in the value of $200,000 and her father received most of her mother's estate. My lawyer obtained a copy of May's Will and probate that showed that Beryl was misleading in her affidavit when she claimed that she received very little from her mother's estate. She had understated the value of her inheritance. She and her father were the executors, and the stated value of the estate that they had written on the probate application was $800,000. This is four times the value that she wrote in her affidavit and much less than the two-million-dollar written offer that a property investor made for May's house shortly after her death. In fact, she had received everything that her mother had owned in her own name outright. She was trying to claim she was hard done by... destitute. A poor little rich girl lamenting her poverty. May's death made Beryl a very wealthy woman!

A Notice to Admit was sent to her to save court time arguing over an issue that could be proven by official documentation. She had to admit that the statement she made in her affidavit was incorrect.

A Notice to Admit was sent to Neville McNaughton where anomalies between the sworn affidavits were pointed out to him. These 'Notices to Admit' were ignored by both parties.

Their lawyer in reply, sent me a Notice to Admit over the people who witnessed the Will signing. I was expected to agree that the friends did witness the Will being signed by Allen and that it was his signature on the final Will. I ignored the notice. I was learning tactics from the best of them.

The Bilk's telephone bills, as well as those of Ralph Daunton were subpoenaed. A letter was sent to the Supreme Court from their lawyer objecting to the requirement for them to produce their telephone bills.

A few days later Ms. Washingham informed Thomas White-Knight that the subpoenaed telephone accounts would be produced and that a forensic document examiner's report would be obtained to show that the signatures on the final Will were in fact Allen's. Neither of these promised items was ever produced.

It was getting close to the 23rd August trial date. Time was running out!

I decided that I was as well prepared as I could be in a legal sense but on a personal note I was nowhere ready. Their lawyer planned on the trial lasting for five days. I would be sitting in a courtroom under the scrutiny of a judge, barristers, lawyers, members of the public and who knows what other people. I had to plan my wardrobe. I wanted to portray a look of simple elegance without looking too pretentious. I was feeling outraged by the denigrating statements made about me. I am well educated with a University degree and I hold down a high position in a good job. I doubted that these attributes would be considered in a court. Everyone would be basing their judgement of me on my appearance. Did I look good enough to convince them that Beryl's statements are untrue? I needed to show that I was a worthy partner for Allen, that he would have been proud to have me by his side, and how I dressed and looked going into that trial would show me at my best. I was feeling trepidation about the unknown but also actually getting quite excited about the prospect of this all being over.

51. A Settlement is Reached

In the background of trial preparation, the settlement negotiations were continuing. On 12th August Beryl and I agreed to a settlement. I was to receive the farm outright, with all stock and plant, plus all my legal costs would be paid. I did not press for my share of the residual estate as I was happy to reach an end, feeling that this settlement was a good outcome. I was told that this was the bottom line for Beryl. She was becoming hardened. I thought that she had already turned to stone. If I pushed my luck and tried to get all that was willed to me in the 2006 Will or held out and went to court, I was sure that a way would be found of delaying again. I did not want to spend another year at this. Beryl and her children were to share in the rest of the estate and she was given permission to apply for probate on any Will that she wished. I agreed that I would not take up my role as executor in any of the previous Wills.

August 20th, 2011 The Deed of Settlement was signed. The trial date was cancelled. The caveat was removed from the probate application. The caveats were removed from the property titles. Beryl could start finalising the estate.

September 5th, 2011 a Supreme Court Order was made that stipulated that within 28 days from the 2nd September Beryl had to transfer the farm title over to me and pay my legal costs.

Six weeks later I was informed that Beryl could not transfer the property to me until she applied for probate. The earlier probate application had been refused so there was no Will probate application on record. Beryl paid the lawyers for all the legal costs associated with the case, as was agreed. The troubles were over for everyone. Or were they?

A few days before Christmas at 1.30am there was a knock on my door. Luke opened the door to find the people who lived in a house near the back of my farm. They were extremely distressed because they almost had an accident while driving past my place. They told us that my cows were out wandering in the street. I went to investigate and to get them back into their paddock. Someone had cut the padlock off the side gate on my farm and blocked it open with a rock to prevent it swinging shut. I could tell by the cow footprints in the mud and the quantity of manure around the gateway that the cows had been deliberately forced out of the gate onto the roadway. I got them back into the paddock. The next day I discovered that there was an enormous quantity of cow footprints overridden by human shoeprints leading along the inside of the fence. It appeared that the cows had been herded down along the inside fence to where the gate was located and then herded out onto the road. Judging by the amount of trampling visible in the soil just inside the gate, it appeared that the cows were reluctant to go out through the gate.

It seemed like some force was required to get them to go out. Maybe a stock whip was used on them! When Luke and I, assisted by the neighbours, herded the cows back they were very willing to return to their paddock through the gate. I reported it to the police later that day. They filed a report but there was not much more that the police could do, as it would be impossible to identify who let the cows out. Only, I had been singled out for this treatment. The property on the opposite side of the road was just as isolated as my property and there was a gate opposite my gate. It was not touched. Those cows were left in their paddock. No one else in the district ever had stock forced out onto the street in the night or at any time during the day. It only happened to me!

Christmas was here again! The property still had not been transferred into my name. Nothing would happen now until the New Year.

In early January, sometime during the night someone rammed a car through the padlocked gate in the side fence. The gate was completely smashed and mangled. The metal catches on the gate were broken. The person drove down through the centre of the farm towards the back of the property. The gates in the dividing paddocks were smashed on the way. The person or persons drove through and smashed the side gate that was located about one hundred metres from the back of the farm. I knew that it had to be someone who knew the property, as it would be very difficult for someone to be able to drive from the front to the back of the farm in the dark, even with the headlights on. There is a track that goes halfway down the farm but then it ends. There is no trail or driveway to show the way to the side gate at the back of the farm. It would be almost impossible to find that gateway in the dark. It is hidden among the trees and blackberry bushes that are growing over the gate and the side fence. The vehicle tracks drove directly to it; they did not meander around like someone looking to find the gateway would have done. Again, only I received this treatment. There was no other property in the district that had anything similar happen to it.

January 12th, 2012 The property title had still not been transferred. A letter was sent to Beryl's lawyer requesting that she comply with the court order within 14 days. There was no reply received from either party.

February 2nd, 2012 Beryl applied for probate on the 2006 Will.

March 15th, 2012, six weeks later we still had not heard anything from Beryl or her lawyers. My lawyer sent a letter to Beryl's lawyer inquiring why probate application was still stopped. In her previous probate application Beryl valued the entire estate, including my farm, at 9.5 million. In her latest probate application, she now valued the estate at 20 million without the inclusion of my farm. I wondered whether this revaluation was causing problems with the probate application She was obviously trying to minimise future tax obligations when she sold any property by placing a high value on the properties that she was inheriting thereby reducing her capital gain from the increase in value after Allen's death.

My lawyers and I discussed issuing enforcement proceedings. The cost of the process was very high and the timeframe for it to take effect would be quite a few months. They advised me to wait a little longer. On the 22nd of March probate was granted, but the property was still not transferred into my name. Beryl's delaying tactics frustrated me. We had agreed on a settlement but I could not move on with my life. In addition, I now had considerable further legal costs to pay that had not been taken into account in the settlement agreement.

Early one morning I received an unusual telephone call. "Hello, I am trying to contact Catherine McLeod the partner of the late Alan Johnson are you her?" Many thoughts ran through my mind. The voice sounded very familiar. Was this some sort of trick being played on me by Beryl and Wayne? I tentatively replied in the affirmative. The caller sighed audibly, "Oh good!" "I am Bob Bilk, Wayne Bilk's brother. 'That explains the familiar voice, I thought.' Bob and Wayne had a falling out over twenty years ago and neither had been on speaking terms since. I had only met Bob once but he shared Wayne's voice. "I have just heard about your legal problems between Beryl, Wayne and you over Alan's will". "My sister and I are having a similar problem with Wayne over our own father's will." "Our father left his entire estate to our mother with the provision that the estate be shared equally between us, his three children, after her death." "Wayne was the executor of the estate." "Our father's estate mostly comprised of a large property portfolio." "It is now all gone!" "Sold!" "By Wane!" "Without our mother's knowledge or consent!" He forged our mother's signature to sell 28 properties belonging to our family trust!" "We have just found out about it." "We are utterly devastated!" "The proceeds from the sale of our properties were used to purchase other real estate solely in Wayne's name." "The money was gifted by Wayne, as the executor of dad's estate, to Wayne for his exclusive use." "We are outraged but our mother refuses to do anything about it." "She said that she would rather be penniless than see one her children go to jail." "You had a similar problem with Alan's estate, didn't you?" "You should have received a much larger share of the estate according to his will but you are not getting it." "We are desperate." "We need your help." "WOULD YOU CONSIDER REOPENING YOUR CASE?"

By this time, we had waited nearly two months since our last contact with Beryl's lawyers and still there has been no response from them so my lawyer sent a letter threatening to reopen the case. The next day Beryl, finally, transferred the farm title into my name. May 5th, 2012, five years and three months had passed since Allen died. This was quite a long time, but it was still half the time that Wayne threatened that he would take. I was the one with the least money in this dispute but this was one case where the one with the most money DID NOT WIN!

The suspect Will with the different signatures is locked away at the probate office. Access to this document is restricted. The Bilks can continue with their life as if the Will saga had never happened. It has been financially rewarding for them, as they ended up with more of the estate than if they hadn't done it, and no resulting consequences inflicted on them. The personal cost may have been high, their own children had to spend five years of their lives in a home that was in a state of conflict. As for Beryl and Wayne, rumour has it that their marriage broke down immediately after the settlement agreement was signed.

A lawyer with whom I was speaking with about the case after it had been finalized commented on the cost of the case. "It sounds to me like a good few private school educations were paid for by that case." I do not know how much was paid to lawyers for their side, but my legal costs came to just over $300,000. I suspect that their costs exceeded this amount, considering the many changes of law firms that they had. Each new firm had to start from the beginning to learn about the situation and the background to the case. I discovered that law firms only passed documents on to the next firm; they didn't seem to give away any background information that they knew about the case or any of their own files. Whenever they changed law firms, my lawyer had to fill the new lawyers in on a lot of the case background information to save on time and my costs. The costs were only for the time spent by lawyers, barristers and specialist witnesses. No accounting was made for the time that I spent writing affidavits and finding evidence to back up my claims. I told my lawyer that I could write a book using all the writing that I had done. My lawyer referred to the book as 'War and Peace' based on the amount of writing it would contain. There wasn't much peace during the case.

While Allen was alive there was one overriding fact that made it impossible for Beryl and Wayne to get him to do what they wanted. Throughout the years leading up to his death I never argued with him. Whenever he had arguments with Beryl and was harassed by Wayne, he knew that his home life with me was peaceful. I never argued with him about the case. I refused to discuss it, and we carried on with our life the same as before the case was initiated. This made it very difficult for them because they had nothing that they could use to turn him against me. Allen, for his part, was always grateful to me for the care that I gave him. After he had died many people told me what he had said to them about me. He claimed that he only managed to live for as long as he did because of the care that I gave, and he wanted to look after me because of this. These people were willing to go to court to attest his acknowledgement of my care for him.

I believe that in this modern age will makers should make a video will explaining the people who are present at the will making and the reasons why the person is distributing his or her assets in the manner of their choosing. It will not stop people litigating over an estate but it will make a lot of issues that could arise post-death easier to resolve.

After the settlement, I ended up with a valuable piece of real estate but no cash to maintain it. I could sell the place outright, but I had attachment issues with the property and did not really want to move. I wanted to continue to live on the property. Due to the delays in the settling of the Will and the Global Financial Crisis, the value of my farm when I finally became the owner was much less than it was at the time of Allen's death. The costs of maintaining the property are very high but the income that I can make off the property cannot cover the holding costs. I am still very well off, although asset rich and cash poor.

The one most important thing missing from my life is my friend, Allen. I would go back in time and change everything if I still had him. Time and the court case, the stalking, the fear has changed me in many ways. It separated me from the memories that should have mattered most and in writing this book I did remember. The love and friendship we shared was everything. It still is.

Every day when I wake up I remember May's words and tell myself, "Today is the first day of the rest of my life! Enjoy it, because

'Dead is Forever!'"

###

If you enjoyed reading about my experience or have suffered through a similar situation and would like to

connect with me:

Email: mail to: cathmac2017@gmail.com

Follow me on Twitter: http://twitter.com/cathmac2017

Friend me on Facebook:
https://www.facebook.com/profile.php?id=100014847849918

Subscribe to my blog:
https://www.blogger.com/blogger.g?blogID=4398846485176906041#allposts

No part of this book may be reproduced in any form, by photocopying or by any electronic or mechanical means, including information storage or retrieval systems, without permission in writing from the Author and the publisher of this book.

This book is based on actual events. The Author has changed names and taken all care to protect the identities of people including identity within scenarios mentioned in this publication.

www.ingramcontent.com/pod-product-compliance
Lightning Source LLC
Chambersburg PA
CBHW051942290426
44110CB00015B/2071